PROBLEMS IN CIVILIZATION

LENIN

Dedicated Marxist or Revolutionary Pragmatist

Edited with
an Introduction by

Stanley W. Page

The City College of
The City University of New York

FORUM PRESS

CONTENTS

INTRODUCTION

In a life marked by Herculean labors and by a single-minded dedication to his purpose, Lenin, a natural leader of enormous strength, breathed new life into a dying belief in the Marxian prophecy. He replaced the tsar as ruler of the vast Russian empire, reorganizing its political and economic structure from top to bottom. In so doing he produced a vision of fulfillment for the world's "prisoners of starvation," to use the phrase made famous by the anthem of the Communist International which he founded in Moscow in March, 1919. Following is a more detailed summary of his life's accomplishments:

In 1900 he was instrumental in establishing the journal *Iskra* as the central organ of the Russian Social Democratic Workers' Party, and he became one of its most prolific writers. By that time the party had generally succeeded in defining its Marxist proletarian orientation as distinct from that of the agrarian socialists, or *narodniki*. Still, Lenin insisted that the Russian Marxist movement required for its success many of the elements traditional to the *narodniki*, including a highly authoritarian and centralized power structure which, by implication, a single man would have to dominate. He was determined to be that man. This meant trying to shift the party away from a relatively moderate revolutionary course that various of his fellow Social Democrats seemed willing to follow, in line with currents then prevailing among the Marxist parties of Europe. The result of this explosive attempt was the split of Russian Marxism, that grew out of the party congress of 1903. The faction following Lenin became known as Bolshevik. Bolshevism, a composite of *narodnichestvo* (populism) and Marxism, was probably more truly Marxian in revolutionary spirit than was Menshevism, the social democratic faction opposing Lenin. By 1905, Lenin had devised a means for bringing the peasants to the side of the workers in the course of the revolution through an elaborate technique of mass manipulation; thereby he further implemented a formula for revolution that was to prove successful well beyond Russia, most notably in China.

Lenin helped to instigate the workers' rising of December 1905 in Moscow, the only manifestation of armed proletarian resistance to the Russian government in that revolutionary year and the first such action in Europe since the days of the Paris Commune. In the difficult years of exile and dispersion of revolutionaries (1907—1912), he was able to keep alive the spirit of Bolshevism among the workers of the Russian Empire. This was amply demonstrated when socialist agitational activities became possible again in 1912, for it was mainly to the Bolshevik banners that most of the urban workers rallied. In the summer of 1914 they erected barricades in St. Petersburg, ready to answer the Bolshevik call and prepared to shed their blood to prevent Russia's entry into World War I — the "imperialist" war, as Lenin was to label it.

In 1915—1916 Lenin composed a pamphlet entitled *Imperialism* that would, in the subsequent half century, help to rouse the impoverished majority of the world's people against the more affluent minority. This paralleled the effect in Europe, during the previous half century, of Marx's *Communist Manifesto*, which incited the working class of that continent against capitalism. Also in the years 1915—1916, Lenin began to call for the formation of a new International that he hoped would end the war among nations by initiating civil war within each of the belligerents and thus give rise to the world revolution. The Second International —most of whose leaders had adopted patriotic stances at the outset of World War I—he effectively exposed as an outright fraud and thereby helped to destroy it.

Returning to Russia in April 1917, he proceeded to undermine the stature of the Provisional Government as well as the moderate socialist leadership by broadcasting the audacious idea that the soviets (councils) of workers and soldiers' deputies, which had been formed spontaneously in March, constituted the natural people's government. Fearing among other things a German seizure of Petrograd, the base from which he hoped to guide the European revolution, Lenin demanded from September 17, 1917 on that his own party take power by forcible means. When the coup d'etat took place in November, he became head of the world's first government committed to socialism and began to restore order to a Russia engulfed since 1916 in ever-deeping chaos. His assumption of power probably saved the Russian Empire from disintegrating into its diverse national parts (as happened shortly thereafter to the Austrian and Ottoman empires and somewhat later to the empires of Britain and France). This was accomplished primarily by extricating Russia from the war with the Central Powers. That bold, if risky, action was carried out by Lenin only after winning a terrific struggle against determined opposition from within his own party.

The three years that followed the signing of the Treaty of Brest-Litovsk with the Central Powers in 1918 saw Lenin pressed to the utmost to preserve his government by defeating many armies of anti-Bolshevik forces—Russian and interventionist—and finally by repelling a Polish invasion. These victories were largely the result of popular response to Lenin's fervent appeals to sacrifice for the defense of the workers' and peasants' revolution. Nevertheless, when the fighting was ended and pragmatism, rather than fanaticism, was required for the survival of the Soviet Republic, Lenin readily about-faced, called off the crusade for communism, laid aside the banners calling for world revolution, and turned his party to the business of providing the means of subsistence for a long-deprived populace.

There in brief, are the facts of Lenin's career, but how to interpret them has caused furious debate. What kind of man was Lenin? Which were his true, which his professed purposes, and how should the means he chose to achieve his aims be evaluated?

Like all figures of history who have altered the order of society and social thinking, Lenin is venerated by some, despised by others. Each side has too great an emotional investment in its particular vision of life to feel any need to know what the real Lenin was like. Therefore, the literature of the opposing camps has sought more to perpetuate a myth than to approach its subject empirically. Even in writings of the "objective center," the needle of the poly-graph wavers, for the writers in question are still too close to Lenin's own time not to feel some emotion about him and cannot escape the polarizations of the cold war.

Furthermore, Lenin was a man of faith—Marxism. Unlike an ordinary religion, his faith had an earthly aim and had to be kept alive. It needed to be modernized constantly in accordance with changing economic and sociopolitical conditions. Steeped in a tradition that considered moral whatever advanced the cause of the Russian revolution (his brother went to the gallows for attempting to kill the tsar) Lenin felt free, as few other Marxists have, to adapt his beliefs to the problems of the moment. Whatever argument he might offer or whatever tactic he might promote was correct if it furthered the cause. "There can be no revolutionary practice without revolutionary theory," was the aphorism Lenin devised and cited frequently to justify his elastic Marxism. And all zigs and zags of his tactical course, the many forward, backward, and sideward motions that marked its progress, have made it immensely difficult for would-be interpreters of Lenin to establish exactly what he was trying to do at any given time. Lenin was quick to abandon bastions of thought or patterns of behavior that had served their purposes but were no longer useful. Writers since his death have had to decide whether in this or that pamphlet, or through one or another political maneuver, he was merely building a temporary bridgehead, destined for abolition at some expedient future date, or whether he had intended to erect a more permanent structure.

An essential part of Lenin's flexible technique was his readiness at any time to engage in alliances for tactical advantage. Lenin had no hesitation about shaking hands with the Devil or about using any and all parties or expediencies that came his way, including many that might not ordinarily have seemed proper for a man who professed to have a well-established set of principles. But too often in his lifetime, and since his death, have such "mariages de convenances" been denounced as betrayals. So, because he may have accepted money from the German government in World War I to expedite the revolution in Russia, there are those who stigmatize Lenin as having been in Germany's pay. But, if he took the money, he did so without any sense of obligation, and he tried his best to use the revolution, although allegedly financed by German money, as a means for overthrowing the German government.

Shapers of historically significant ideas can seldom be properly understood without an awareness that their views changed in the course of their lives. To read Marx of the 1840s is to examine a landscape of ideas that differs considerably from that of the same author in the 1870s. Marx modified some of his earlier attitudes because of his own growth and because of the way certain of his postulations worked out in the course of time. Followers of any historical trailblazer who have remained satisfied with a position taken by the master in one period of his work will of course see him differently from those who have studied the entire course of the development of his thinking.

In the case of Lenin this situation exists in an exaggerated form. Lenin's earlier views were centered around the problems confronting an illegal party struggling to overthrow the tsarist regime; subsequently he saw himself as the leader of a world revolution, and in his final years he became mainly concerned with the problems of Soviet Russia. Various Communist regimes, whose nations have recently emerged from imperialist domination, and who consider a changed world an essential part of their doctrine, have tended to fix on the ideas of the earlier and fiercer Lenin. But Lenin's heirs in the Soviet Union, having wished for the most part to stress his moderation and his professed desire for peaceful coexistence, have tended to stress the later writings of the Soviet state's founding father. Every shift in Soviet policy since Lenin's death has required the Russian party to highlight whatever aspect of Lenin's teachings seemed best to support it. In a similarly eclectic fashion the communist parties of other countries have drawn from Lenin that which suited the national context within which they functioned. All of this has frequently led writers to confuse Lenin with positions ascribed to him.

Unlike most of history's great prophets, Lenin was not an armchair theoretician but a political activist *par excellence.* Many of those who have written about Lenin knew him first and foremost as a dynamic leader who gave speeches, wrote propaganda, devised slogans, arranged for and supervised conferences and congresses, helped to shape military policy, wrote decrees, and more. These persons who were close to the active Lenin tend to describe him principally in the narrow terms of their own contacts with him. Frequently they have not troubled to read what he wrote, thinking they knew all his thoughts, having shared the experiences that produced them. But they have often been mistaken.

Others who have written about Lenin, among them the superficial scholars and journalists who have had to write an article or a book have simply not taken the time to study Lenin before setting down their erroneous opinions as historic data. All told, many different interpretations of Lenin's meanings have, since 1917, been broadcast throughout the world.

The sheer immensity of Lenin's activity, both as writer and as politician, explains in large part why there is as yet no adequate biography of Lenin. Nevertheless, some of Lenin's biographers to date have successfully struck upon aspects of Lenin's thought, work, or personality that are generally sound. Part of this volume's purpose is to cull that which is worthwhile from among the best that has been written about this great figure of world history and thereby present the student with materials from which he may construct as true as possible a representation, given the space limitations of a book such as this.

The single major reason for the widely disparate views on Lenin is the fact that almost every one of his actions—because of their immense historic or contemporary importance—are forever being put to the test of value judgments. Such judgments vary inescapably in accordance with the ideological position of the critic as well as in accordance with what he is trying to judge. Is he judging an action of Lenin as good or bad for humanity as a whole; good or bad for his own country or Lenin's; or good or bad with respect to the success of Lenin's cause and party? What one observer may think to have been a policy proper for the promotion of the cause, may in his, or in someone else's opinion, have harmed Russia. Something that benefited humanity might have harmed the party, or vice versa.

The task of rendering value judgments upon any historic figure is at best a tricky one, but the passing of judgments upon Lenin is more than normally difficult because Lenin appeared to demand so little for himself. Whatever issues he sought to resolve, whatever battles he sought to win, whatever victories he attained never appeared to offer any benefit to Lenin personally. He invariably tried to establish himself in positions of power, but was it power for its own sake or was it power needed to accomplish his revolutionary purposes?

Following is a small sampling of the kinds of positions taken by Lenin that demand subtle inquiry before evaluations can be made:

When, in the period 1901–1903, Lenin strove to compel the organization of the Russian Marxist party along elitist dictatorial lines, was he motivated by a quest for power or was he merely being realistic about the kind of struggle the revolution would require and the kind of leadership such a struggle would demand?

When, in 1905, Lenin worked out a seemingly cynical formula for allying his "Marxist" party with the peasantry in the hoped-for establishment of a revolutionary dictatorship of proletarians and peasants (the toiling masses), was he planning merely to manipulate the peasants, or was he actually trying to gain their support in accomplishing the ends that they themselves should have desired? Would not the coming of industry turn peasants into proletarians? And would not, therefore, the support given by peasants to the proletariat be a service to their own ultimate interests?

When Lenin insisted that Bolsheviks run for seats in the Third Duma and later, in 1920, urged communists to enter bourgeois parliaments and trade unions, was he betraying Marxian principle, or was he simply seeking to establish centers of propaganda through which the masses could most easily remain informed of the Bolshevik position?

Whatever things Lenin did or sanctioned in the first years of Soviet power—including the wholesale murder of innocents, the rigging of elections, the stifling of all opposition such as that evinced in the idealistic struggle waged by the Kronstadt sailors, and even by introducing the N.E.P. and seemingly turning his back on Marxism—were not all these things done to save his government? Because in the long run, that meant saving Marxism and preserving hope for the coming of the world revolution.

The title of this book, *Lenin: Dedicated Marxist or Revolutionary Pragmatist?*, defines the two important points of view (not necessarily contradictory) that are held by those who have written extensively on Lenin. However, for purposes of greater clarity and because Lenin's pragmatism was sometimes a course of action aimed at achieving a base of power and sometimes an action taken from a previously established base, I have divided this volume into three sections.

Marxism, it should be kept in mind, is primarily theory and not the guide to revolutionary action that Lenin often claimed it to be. This theory has virtually nothing to say about how a revolution should be led, and if it makes some mention about the need for establishing a workers' party and a workers' state, it does little to explain these concepts. But Lenin was deeply concerned with the problem of how the revolution was to be carried out in practice, and to him the establishment of such revolutionary bastions of power as a workers' party and a revolutionary state had the significance of essential way stations on the march to the triumph of the socialist revolution. It is interesting to note that among all of history's Marxist leaders only those who followed Lenin (as in China, Yugoslavia, Cuba, Vietnam, Cambodia, and elsewhere) have been able to communize their countries' social and political structure. So although Lenin was a Marxist, he was also an acute tactician of revolution and a technician of power. This book is organized along the lines of these three divisions. The category of each reading has been decided in terms of which of these three themes its author stressed most heavily.

Section One of the book, which deals with Lenin as a dedicated Marxist, is of Bolshevik authorship. For it was only the Bolsheviks who did and still do consider Lenin a dedicated Marxist. The opening reading is Lenin's own exposition of Marxism, as written for an encyclopedia article. The selection from Stalin derives originally from his famous Foundations of

Leninism lectures, given in April and May of 1924, shortly after Lenin's death in January. The purpose of the lectures was to prove that Stalin, and his aims of the moment, were truly in the Lenin mold. Stalin, in trying to demonstrate that Lenin had in no way strayed from Marxism, was trying also to explain that he, Stalin, was working fully within the noble tradition. In the process Lenin inevitably took on some of the coloration of Stalin. Bukharin, having often crossed polemical swords with Lenin, proves in his eulogy of the dead leader that he has finally come to accept Lenin's pragmatic brand of Marxism as a valid interpretation. Klara Zetkin's reminiscences of Lenin's views on women, marriage, and sex faithfully reflect Marx's hostility to the moral hypocrisy of Victorian England which permitted the gentlemen of the bourgeoisie to exploit their wives as instruments of production and allowed them to take unfair advantage of women of the lower class. But Lenin, the austere revolutionary, fearful of indulging in pleasure lest he squander energies that belonged to the cause, is also mirrored. I. Korotkov's summation of Lenin's thoughts on war is a tribute to Lenin's creative Marxism. All strands of Lenin's argument are derived from Marx, but Lenin has woven them into a new conception. The idea of war as an extension of politics to the battlefield is the first enunciation of the cold war, the twentieth century's most pervasive malady.

Section Two of the book deals with Lenin as a tactician of revolution. Max Eastman properly credits Lenin with having added to Marxism the vital dimension of how the prophecy was to be carried to fulfilment. My own article studies Lenin's flexibility, in particular his knack for looking eastward as well as westward, for signs that world revolution was in progress, something the traditionally westward-looking Marxist would never have thought of doing. Lenin's great manipulative talents are well demonstrated by Alfreds Berzins, who examines the devices utilized by Lenin in preventing the great capitalist powers from combining their forces to crush the newborn socialist state which they so greatly feared. A skillful cataloguing, in short compass, of Lenin's tactical tricks en route to power, is the outstanding feature of John Keep's comprehensive essay. An important aspect of Lenin's own ideas on tactics concludes this section.

Section Three contains readings that deal with Lenin's preoccupation with the mechanics of power. If leading Marxists before 1917 seldom thought in terms of holding or even of taking power, that was because they were believers in economic determinism. If, as Marx believed, humanity was inevitably destined to socialism, what mattered the voluntarist acts of an individual, or of a party, or even of a revolutionary state? But Lenin, rooted in the Russian, as well as in the Marxian, revolutionary traditions, arrived at the conviction that a revolution could be made only by a centralized party of ascetic radicals, who, having seized state power, would use that power dictatorially for the purpose of transforming Russian society. Once that was accomplished, Lenin would attempt, through the Communist International, to graft the methods successful in Russia onto the Marxist movement of the entire world.

Adam B. Ulam discusses the sensibleness of Lenin's demand for a revolutionary party that would be short on talk, long on action. Nikolai Valentinov recalls the Lenin of 1904, when the latter was expounding the virtues of Jacobinist centralism and had no qualms about admitting that he alone had the qualities suitable for party leadership. These early attitudes were, according to Bertram D. Wolfe, carried over into the period of Bolshevik state power and marked the beginning of modern totalitarianism. The brief selections from Maxim Gorky's *New Life* and Louis Fisher's biography further suggest that Lenin was a tyrant by nature and inclination. The kind of despot he was may be judged from his article on Bolshevik power, composed shortly before that power was actually attained. Trotsky, because of Lenin's supercentralism, had shied away from Bolshevism until 1917. But his biographical sketch of Lenin, written in 1924, indicates his full acceptance of the need for the dictatorial devices that Lenin introduced in giving structure to a hitherto unknown kind of state that rules in the name of workers and peasants who were, for the most part, illiterate. That Lenin was a reluctant dictator, a dictator by necessity rather than by choice, is the argument presented by Moshe Lewin. The selection from Alfred G. Meyer describes Lenin's skill in balancing the fragile equilibrium between those who desire a revolution but understand nothing about the organizing process, and their leader-organizer and his need, at all times and under all conditions, to enjoy the support of the popular masses.

After studying the selections with their differing emphases, how do you view Lenin? Was he first and foremost a Marxist? Or was he a genius in revolutionary leadership? To put the question another way, did Marxism shape the revolutionary, or was Marxism an incidental, or even accidental, element in Lenin's drive to power? Or, finally, was Lenin such a many-sided man that it is impossible to categorize him simply?

CONFLICT OF OPINION

To Lenin, Marxism was a body of thought infinitely adaptable to all possible situations and constantly evolving to fit the requirements of ever-changing conditions. "It is necessary," Lenin wrote, "to acquire that incontestable truth that a Marxist must take cognizance of living life, of the true facts of reality, that he must not cling to the theory of yesterday." The opinions of Lenin's Bolshevik followers reflect some of the facets of this conception.

> Lenin contributed something new to the general treasury of Marxism as compared with what was created by Marx and Engels, with what could be created in the pre-imperialist period of capitalism; at the same time Lenin's new contribution to the treasury of Marxism is wholly and completely based on the principles laid down by Marx and Engels.
>
> JOSEPH STALIN

> Splendid Marxist that [Lenin] was, he grasped the particular wherever and in whatever form it revealed itself, in its relation to and its bearing upon the whole. . . . Needless to say he saw full social equality of women as a principle which no Communist could dispute.
>
> KLARA ZETKIN

> War, Lenin explained, is a continuation of politics, and in order to understand war one must correctly understand politics, which boil down to relations between classes.
>
> I. KOROTKOV

> Lenin wielded the Marxist weapon in a masterly way. Lenin never allowed it to get cool or remain motionless. It was always a really powerful instrument, which, in Lenin's hands, was turned round to one side or to the other according to the demands of *practical actuality*. It was the Marxism which, vulgarly speaking, has nothing sacred except the interests of the social revolution.
>
> NIKOLAI BUKHARIN

However, Lenin's endless adjustments and shifts of policy in pursuit of revolution seem more than merely Marxist adaptations. Can Lenin's obvious tactical genius be seen independent of his Marxism?

> To me the fundamental difference between Marx and Lenin is visible on almost every page they wrote. It is not a contradiction, but a difference of mental attitude. And it is not a complete difference, because Marx had in him the practical scientist, and Lenin never consciously got rid of the metaphysician. . . . Marx states that such a thing will happen in such a way. Lenin states that such is the only way to make it happen.
>
> MAX EASTMAN

> Lenin had studied the dominant urge of the capitalist world . . . the profit motive, as carefully as he had studied Marxism. . . . This knowledge Lenin used to extreme advantage during the insecure early period of the communist revolution. . . . The capitalists' greed for profit had to be aroused so that they would forget for a time their aversion to communist ideology and methods. That was Lenin's philosophy of action. He proposed to achieve this goal by offering concessions to the capitalists even if this meant letting them have the lion's share for a while.
>
> ALFREDS BERZINS

When it was clear that the Russian Revolution had not set off revolution in the West, Lenin turned his hopes upon the restless stirrings of Asia, where, industry or no industry, world revolution was actually in the making.

STANLEY W. PAGE

Whatever Lenin's merits as a philosopher, historian or literary critic, he was pre-eminently a politician, and it was as a master of political tactics, who skillfully manipulated men and ideas to achieve power for his party, that he won his greatest success.

JOHN KEEP

In order to achieve world-wide social change, Lenin considered it essential to discipline himself, his party, his government and the masses whom he brought under his control. Disagreement centers on the question: Was Lenin dictatorial by nature or by force of political necessity?

Here, as early as 1902, is Lenin's whole schema: the dictatorship of the party over all classes of society, the transmission belt system of implementing that dictatorship, the rule of the many and most diverse groups by the fewest and most homogeneous, the transformation of the authority of ideas into the authority of power in all the manifold activities which were to concern the party—and which activities were not?

BERTRAM D. WOLFE

Lenin is one of the most striking figures of international social democracy; a man of talent, he possesses all the qualities of a "leader" and also the lack of morality necessary for this role, as well as an utterly pitiless attitude . . . toward the lives of the popular masses.

MAXIM GORKY

"The proletarian state," Lenin asserted, "will begin to wither away immediately after its victory. . . ." The failure of communist states to follow the . . . withering away blueprint flows from Lenin's mistaken notion that a proletarian revolution would create "a society without class antagonisms. . . ." Lenin's *The State and Revolution* lies in the museum, . . . mocked by the revolution, . . . scrapped by its revolutionary author. . . . Life killed a beautiful theory. Instead of the death of the state, the death of *The State and Revolution*.

LOUIS FISCHER

If in the end Lenin's regime came to be based on force—the bureaucracy, which he abhorred—it was only the result of a situation in which a program of development is imposed by a new regime on a backward country whose vital social forces are either weak, indifferent or hostile.

MOSHE LEWIN

I. DEDICATED MARXIST

V. I. Lenin

TEACHER OF MARXISM

Lenin was proud to acknowledge that Karl Marx was the source of most of his wisdom (Friedrich Engels should be mentioned in the same breath) and the name of Marx was perpetually on the tip of his tongue or pen. Believing himself to be the sole true apostle, Lenin considered it his life's mission to bring to his generation of proletarians the master's teachings intact and unsullied by others who had "vulgarized" Marx. The following is extracted from an encyclopedia article on Marx's life and teachings that Lenin completed in November, 1914. It is notable for its succinctness and lucidity.

MARXISM is the system of the views and teachings of Marx. Marx was the genius who continued and completed the three main ideological currents of the nineteenth century, belonging to the three most advanced countries of mankind: classical German philosophy, classical English political economy, and French Socialism together with French revolutionary doctrines in general. The remarkable consistency and integrity of Marx's views, acknowledged even by his opponents, views which in their totality constitute modern materialism and modern scientific Socialism, as the theory and program of the labour movement in all the civilized countries of the world, oblige us to present a brief outline of his world-conception in general before proceeding to the exposition of the principal content of Marxism, namely, Marx's economic doctrine.

* * *

THE MATERIALIST CONCEPTION OF HISTORY

Having realized the inconsistency, incompleteness, and onesidedness of the old materialism, Marx became convinced of the necessity of "bringing the science of society . . . into harmony with the materialist foundation, and of reconstructing it thereupon." Since materialism in general explains consciousness as the outcome of being, and not conversely, materialism as applied to the social life of mankind has to explain *social* consciousness as the outcome of *social* being. "Technology," writes Marx (*Capital*, Vol. I), "discloses man's mode of dealing with nature, the process of production by which he sustains his life, and thereby also lays bare the mode of formation of his social relations, and of the mental conceptions that flow from them.". . .

The discovery of the materialist conception of history, or rather, the consistent continuation, extension of materialism to the domain of social phenomena, removed two of the chief defects of earlier historical theories. In the first place, they at best examined only the ideological motives of the historical activity of human beings, without investigating what produced these motives, without grasping the objective laws governing the development of the system of social relations, and without discerning the roots of these relations in the degree of development of material production; in the second place it was precisely the activities of the *masses* of the population

From V. I. Lenin, *Marx, Engels, M   ɔw: Foreign Languages Publishing House, 1947),
pp. 19, 24–34, 41–44. Footnotes in   ɟuent selections have been omitted.

that the earlier theories did not cover, whereas historical materialism made it possible for the first time to study with the accuracy of the natural sciences the social conditions of the life of the masses and the changes in these conditions. Pre-Marxian "sociology" and historiography *at best* provided an accumulation of raw facts, collected at random, and a depiction of certain sides of the historical process. By examining the *ensemble* of all the opposing tendencies, by reducing them to precisely definable conditions of life and production of the various *classes* of society, by discarding subjectivism and arbitrariness in the choice of various "leading" ideas or in their interpretation, and by disclosing that all ideas and all the various tendencies, without exception, have their *roots* in the condition of the material forces of production, Marxism pointed the way to an all-embracing and comprehensive study of the process of the genesis, development, and decline of social-economic formations. People make their own history. But what determines the motives of people, of the mass of people, that is; what gives rise to the clash of conflicting ideas and strivings; what is the ensemble of all these clashes of the whole mass of human societies; what are the objective conditions of production of material life that form the basis of all historical activity of man; what is the law of development of these conditions—to all this Marx drew attention and pointed out the way to a scientific study of history as a uniform and law-governed process in all its immense variety and contradictoriness.

THE CLASS STRUGGLE

That in any given society the strivings of some of its members conflict with the strivings of others, that social life is full of contradictions, that history discloses a struggle within nations and societies as well as between nations and societies, and, in addition, an alternation of periods of revolution and reaction, peace and war, stagnation and rapid progress or decline—are facts that are generally known. Marxism provided the clue which enables us to discover the laws governing this seeming labyrinth and chaos, namely, the theory of the class struggle. Only a study of the ensemble of strivings of all the members of a given society or group of societies can lead to a scientific definition of the result of these strivings. And the source of the conflict of strivings lies in the differences in the position and mode of life of the *classes* into which each society is divided. "The history of all hitherto existing society is the history of class struggles," wrote Marx in the *Communist Manifesto* (except the history of the primitive community—Engels added). "Freeman and slave, patrician and plebeian, lord and serf, guild-master and journeyman, in a word, oppressor and oppressed, stood in constant opposition to one another, carried on an uninterrupted, now hidden, now open fight, a fight that each time ended, either in a revolutionary reconstitution of society at large, or in the common ruin of the contending classes. . . . The modern bourgeois society that has sprouted from the ruins of feudal society has not done away with class antagonisms. It has but established new classes, new conditions of oppression, new forms of struggle in place of the old ones. Our epoch, the epoch of the bourgeoisie, possesses, however, this distinctive feature: It has simplified the class antagonisms. Society as a whole is more and more splitting up into two great hostile camps, into two great classes directly facing each other—bourgeoisie and proletariat." Ever since the Great French Revolution, European history has very clearly revealed in a number of countries this real undersurface of events, the struggle of classes. And the Restoration period in France already produced a number of historians (Thierry, Guizot, Mignet, Thiers) who, generalizing from events, could not but recognize that the class struggle was the key to all French history. And the modern era—the era of the complete victory of the bourgeoisie, representative institutions, wide (if not universal) suffrage, a cheap, popular daily press, etc., the era of powerful and ever-expanding unions of workers and unions of employers, etc.—has revealed even more manifestly (though sometimes in a very one-sided, "peaceful," "constitutional" form) that the class struggle is the mainspring of events. The following passage from Marx's *Communist Manifesto* will show us what Marx required of social science in respect to an objective analysis of the position of each class in modern society in connection with an analysis of the conditions of development of each class:

Of all the classes that stand face to face with the bourgeoisie today, the proletariat alone is a really revolutionary class. The other classes decay and finally disappear in the face of modern industry; the proletariat is its special and essential product. The lower middle class: the small manufacturer, the shopkeeper, the artisan, the peasant—all these fight against the bourgeoisie, to save from extinction their existence as fractions of the middle class. They are therefore not revolutionary, but conservative. Nay more, they are reactionary, for they try to roll back the wheel of history. If by chance they are revolutionary, they are so only in view of their impending transfer into the proletariat; they thus defend not their present, but their future interests; they desert their own standpoint to place themselves at that of the proletariat.

In a number of historic works, Marx has given us brilliant and profound examples of materialist historiography, of an analysis of the position of *each* individual class, and sometimes of various groups or strata within a class, showing plainly why and how "every class struggle is a political struggle." The above-quoted passage is an illustration of what a complex network of social relations and *transitional* stages between one class and another, from the past to the future, Marx analyses in order to determine the result of historical development.

The most profound, comprehensive and detailed confirmation and application of Marx's theory is his economic doctrine.

MARX'S ECONOMIC DOCTRINE

"It is the ultimate aim of this work to lay bare the economic law of motion of modern society" (that is to say, capitalist, bourgeois society), says Marx in the preface to *Capital*. The investigation of the relations of production in a given, historically defined society, in their genesis, development, and decline—such is the content of Marx's economic doctrine. In capitalist society it is the production of *commodities* that dominates, and Marx's analysis therefore begins with an analysis of the commodity.

Value

A commodity is, in the first place, a thing that satisfies a human want; in the second place, it is a thing that can be exchanged for another thing. The utility of a thing makes it a *use-value*. Exchange-value (or simply, value) presents itself first of all as a relation, as the proportion in which a certain number of use-values of one sort are exchanged for a certain number of use-values of another sort. Daily experience shows us that millions upon millions of such exchanges are constantly equating one with another every kind of use-value, even the most diverse and incomparable. Now, what is there in common between these various things, things constantly equated one with another in a definite system of social relations? What is common to them is that they are *products of labour*. In exchanging products people equate to one another the most diverse kinds of labour. The production of commodities is a system of social relations in which the single producers create diverse products (the social division of labour), and in which all these products are equated to one another in exchange. Consequently, what is common to all commodities is not the concrete labour of a definite branch of production, not labour of one particular kind, but *abstract* human labour—human labour in general. All the labour power of a given society, as represented in the sum total of values of all commodities, is one and the same human labour power; millions and millions of acts of exchange prove this. And, consequently, each particular commodity represents only a certain share of the *socially necessary* labour time. The magnitude of value is determined by the amount of socially necessary labour, or by the labour time that is socially necessary for the production of the given commodity, of the given use-value. ". . . Whenever, by an exchange, we equate as values our different products, by that very act, we also equate, as human labour, the different kinds of labour expended upon them. We are not aware of this, nevertheless we do it." As one of the earlier economists said, value is a relation between two persons; only he ought to have added: a relation screened by a material integument. We can understand what value is only when we consider it from the standpoint of the system of social relations of production of one particular historical formation of society, relations, moreover, which manifest themselves in the mass phenomenon of exchange, a phenomenon which repeats itself millions upon millions of times. "As values, all commodities are only definite masses of congealed labour time." Having made a detailed analysis of the twofold character of the labour incorporated in commodities, Marx goes on to analyse the *forms of value* and *money*. Marx's main task here is to study the *origin* of the money form of value, to study the *historical process* of development of exchange, from isolated and casual acts of exchange ("elementary or accidental form of value," in which a given quantity of one commodity is exchanged for a given quantity of another) to the universal form of value, in which a number of different commodities are exchanged for one and the same particular commodity, and to the money form of value, when gold becomes this particular commodity, the universal equivalent. Being the highest product of the development of exchange and commodity production, money masks and conceals the social character of private labour, the social tie between the individual producers who are united by the market. Marx analyses in great detail the various functions of money; and it is essential to note here in particular (as generally in the opening chapters of *Capital*) that the abstract and seemingly at times purely deductive mode of exposition in reality reproduces a gigantic collection of factual material on the history of the development of exchange and

commodity production. ". . . If we consider money, its existence implies a definite stage in the exchange of commodities. The particular functions of money which it performs, either as the mere equivalent of commodities, or as means of circulation, or means of payment, as hoard or as universal money, point, according to the extent and relative preponderance of the one function or the other, to very different stages in the process of social production."

Surplus Value

At a certain stage in the development of commodity production money becomes transformed into capital. The formula of commodity circulation was C—M—C (commodity—money—commodity), *i.e.*, the sale of one commodity for the purpose of buying another. The general formula of capital, on the contrary, is M—C—M (money—commodity—money), *i.e.*, purchase for the purpose of selling (at a profit). The increase over the original value of money put into circulation Marx calls surplus value. The fact of this "growth" of money in capitalist circulation is well known. It is this "growth" which transforms money into *capital*, as a special, historically defined, social relation of production. Surplus value cannot arise out of commodity circulation, for the latter knows only the exchange of equivalents; it cannot arise out of an addition to price, for the mutual losses and gains of buyers and sellers would equalize one another, whereas what we have here is not an individual phenomenon but a mass, average, social phenomenon. In order to derive surplus value, the owner of money "must . . . find . . . in the market a commodity whose use-value possesses the peculiar property of being a source of value"—a commodity whose process of consumption is at the same time a process of creation of value. And such a commodity exists. It is human labour power. Its consumption is labour, and labour creates value. The owner of money buys labour power at its value, which, like the value of every other commodity, is determined by the socially necessary labour time requisite for its production (*i.e.*, the cost of maintaining the worker and his family). Having bought labour power, the owner of money is entitled to use it, that is, to set it to work, for the whole day—twelve hours, let us suppose. Yet, in the course of six hours ("necessary" labour time) the labourer produces product sufficient to cover the cost of his own maintenance; and in the course of the next six hours ("surplus" labour time), he produces "surplus" product, or surplus value, for which the capitalist does not pay. In capital, therefore, from the standpoint of the process of production, two parts must be distinguished: constant capital, expended on means of production (machinery, tools, raw materials, etc.), the value of which, without any change, is transferred (all at once or part by part) to the finished product; and variable capital, expended on labour power. The value of this latter capital is not invariable, but grows in the labour process, creating surplus value. Therefore, to express the degree of exploitation of labour power by capital, surplus value must be compared not with the whole capital but only with the variable capital. Thus in the example given, the rate of surplus value, as Marx calls this ratio, will be 6:6, *i.e.*, 100 per cent.

The historical conditions necessary for the genesis of capital were, firstly, the accumulation of a certain sum of money in the hands of individuals and a relatively high level of development of commodity production in general, and, secondly, the existence of a labourer who is "free" in a double sense: free from all constraint or restriction on the sale of his labour power, and free from the land and all means of production in general, a free and unattached labourer, a "proletarian," who cannot subsist except by the sale of his labour power.

There are two principal methods by which surplus value can be increased: by lengthening the working day ("absolute surplus value"), and by shortening the necessary working day ("relative surplus value"). Analysing the first method, Marx gives a most impressive picture of the struggle of the working class to shorten the working day and of governmental interference to lengthen the working day (from the fourteenth century to the seventeenth century) and to shorten the working day (factory legislation of the nineteenth century). Since the appearance of *Capital*, the history of the working-class movement in all civilized countries of the world has provided a wealth of new facts amplifying this picture.

Analysing the production of relative surplus value, Marx investigates the three main historical stages by which capitalism has increased the productivity of labour: (1) simple co-operation; (2) division of labour and manufacture; (3) machinery and large-scale industry. How profoundly Marx has here revealed the basic and typical features of capitalist development is incidentally shown by the fact that investigations of what is known as the "kustar" [home] industry of Russia furnish abundant material illustrating the first two of the mentioned stages. And the revolutionizing effect of large-scale machine industry, described by Marx in 1867, has been revealed in a number of "new" countries (Russia, Japan, etc.) in the course of the half-century that has since elapsed.

To continue. New and important in the highest degree is Marx's analysis of the *accumulation of capital*, *i.e.*, the transformation of a part of surplus value into capital, its use, not for satisfying the personal needs or whims of the capitalist, but for new production. Marx revealed the mistake of all the earlier, classical political economists (from Adam Smith on), who assumed that the entire surplus value which is transformed into capital goes to form variable capital. In actual fact, it is divided into *means of production* and variable capital. Of tremendous importance to the process of development of capitalism and its transformation into Socialism is the more rapid growth of the constant capital share (of the total capital) as compared with the variable capital share.

The accumulation of capital, by accelerating the replacement of workers by machinery and creating wealth at one pole and poverty at the other, also gives rise to what is called the "reserve army of labour," to the "relative surplus" of workers, or "capitalist overpopulation," which assumes the most diverse forms and enables capital to expand production at an extremely fast rate. This, in conjunction with credit facilities and the accumulation of capital in the means of production, incidentally furnishes the clue to the *crises* of overproduction that occur periodically in capitalist countries—at first at an average of every ten years, and later at more lengthy and less definite intervals. From the accumulation of capital under capitalism must be distinguished what is known as primitive accumulation: the forcible divorcement of the worker from the means of production, the driving of the peasants from the land, the stealing of the commons, the system of colonies and national debts, protective tariffs, and the like. "Primitive accumulation" creates the "free" proletarian at one pole, and the owner of money, the capitalist, at the other.

* * *

SOCIALISM

From the foregoing it is evident that Marx deduces the inevitability of the transformation of capitalist society into Socialist society wholly and exclusively from the economic law of motion of contemporary society. The socialization of labour, which is advancing ever more rapidly in thousands of forms, and which has manifested itself very strikingly during the half-century that has elapsed since the death of Marx in the growth of large-scale production, capitalist cartels, syndicates and trusts, as well as in the gigantic increase in the dimensions and power of finance capital, forms the chief material foundation for the inevitable coming of Socialism. The intellectual and moral driving force and the physical executant of this transformation is the proletariat, which is trained by capitalism itself. The struggle of the proletariat against the bourgeoisie, which manifests itself in various and, as to its content, increasingly richer forms, inevitably becomes a political struggle aiming at the conquest of political power by the proletariat ("the dictatorship of the proletariat"). The socialization of production is bound to lead to the conversion of the means of production into the property of society, to the "expropriation of the expropriators." This conversion will directly result in an immense increase in productivity of labour, a reduction of working hours, and the replacement of the remnants, the ruins of small-scale, primitive, disunited production by collective and improved labour. Capitalism finally snaps the bond between agriculture and industry; but at the same time, in its highest development it prepares new elements of this bond, of a union between industry and agriculture based on the conscious application of science and the combination of collective labour, and on a redistribution of the human population (putting an end at one and the same time to the rural remoteness, isolation and barbarism, and to the unnatural concentration of vast masses of people in big cities). A new form of family, new conditions in the status of women and in the upbringing of the younger generation are being prepared by the highest forms of modern capitalism: female and child labour and the break-up of the patriarchal family by capitalism inevitably assume the most terrible, disastrous, and repulsive forms in modern society. Nevertheless ". . . modern industry, by assigning as it does an important part in the process of production, outside the domestic sphere, to women, to young persons, and to children of both sexes, creates a new economical foundation for a higher form of the family and of the relations between the sexes. It is, of course, just as absurd to hold the Teutonic-Christian form of the family to be absolute and final as it would be to apply that character to the ancient Roman, the ancient Greek, or the Eastern forms which, moreover, taken together form a series in historic development. Moreover, it is obvious that the fact of the collective working group being composed of individuals of both sexes and all ages, must necessarily, under suitable conditions, become a source of humane development: although in its spontaneously developed, brutal, capitalistic form, where the labourer exists for the process of production, and not the process of production for the labourer, that fact is a pestiferous source of corruption and slavery." In the factory system is to be found "the germ of the education of the future, an education that will, in the case of every child over a given age, combine productive labour with instruction and gymnastics, not only as one of the methods of adding to the efficiency of production, but as the only method of producing fully developed human beings."

Marxian Socialism puts the question of nationality and of the state on the same historical footing, not only in the sense of explaining the past but also in the sense of a fearless forecast of the future and of bold practical action for its achievement. Nations are an inevitable product, an inevitable form in the bourgeois epoch of social development. The working class could not grow strong, could not become mature and formed without "constituting itself within the nation," without being "national" ("though not in the bourgeois sense of the word"). But the development of capitalism more and more breaks down national barriers, destroys national seclusion, substitutes class antagonisms for national antagonisms. It is, therefore, perfectly true that in the developed capitalist countries "the working men have no country" and that "united action" of the workers, of the civilized countries at least, "is one of the first conditions for the emancipation of the proletariat." The state, which is organized violence, inevitably came into being at a definite stage in the development of society, when society had split into irreconcilable classes, and when it could not exist without an "authority" ostensibly standing above society and to a certain degree separate from society. Arising out of class contradictions, the state becomes "the state of the most powerful class, the class which rules in economics and with its aid becomes also the class which rules in politics, and thus acquires new means of holding down and exploiting the oppressed class. Thus, the state of antiquity was primarily the state of the slaveowners for the purpose of holding down the slaves, as the feudal state was the organ of the nobility for holding down the peasant serfs and bondsmen, and the modern representative state is a tool for the exploitation of wage-labour by capital." (Engels, *The Origin of the Family, Private Property and the State*, a work in which the writer expounds his own and Marx's views.) Even the freest and most progressive form of the bourgeois state, the democratic republic, in no way removes this fact, but merely changes its form (connection between the government and the stock exchange, corruption—direct and indirect—of the officialdom and the press, etc.). Socialism, by leading to the abolition of classes, will thereby lead to the abolition of the state.

Joseph Stalin

MODERNIZER OF MARXISM

Joseph Stalin's first contact with Lenin came at the 1905 Bolshevik conference in Tammerfors which he attended as a Bolshevik delegate from the Caucasus. In the subsequent history of the Bolshevik party, until the time of Lenin's death in January of 1924, Stalin ranked as a second-rate figure, usually performing some vital but little applauded task or holding some key position in the party or the Soviet government while remaining well out of the limelight. When he was appointed the party's General Secretary in 1922, from which office he rose to dictator of the U.S.S.R and much of Eastern Europe, he was still some years away from achieving recognition as one of the giants of the communist movement. His slow rise may be attributed in part to his inability to debate questions of Marxist theory on a level with men such as Lenin, Kamenev, Bukharin, and Trotsky. Nevertheless, he is frequently credited with being Lenin's true spiritual successor, a claim Stalin himself never tired of making. All of Lenin's comrades-in-arms considered themselves to be adepts at Marxism, but Stalin was the first among them to recognize that Leninism was equally worth mastering. He, better than all the others, understood the extent to which Marxism, through the person of Lenin, had been adapted to Russia and, by extension, to other underdeveloped countries of the twentieth century.

INTERVIEW WITH THE FIRST AMERICAN LABOUR DELEGATION
September 9, 1927

FIRST QUESTION: What new principles have Lenin and the Communist Party added in practice to Marxism? Would it be correct to say that Lenin believed in "creative revolution" whereas Marx was more inclined to wait for the culmination of the development of economic forces?

ANSWER: I think that Lenin "added" no "new principles" to Marxism, nor did he abolish any of the "old" principles of Marxism. Lenin was, and remains, the most loyal and consistent pupil of Marx and Engels, and he wholly and completely based himself on the principles of Marxism.

But Lenin did not merely carry out the teaching of Marx and Engels. He was at the same time the continuer of that teaching.

What does that mean?

It means that he developed further the teaching of Marx and Engels in conformity with the new conditions of development, with the new phase of capitalism, with imperialism. It means that in developing further the teaching of Marx in the new conditions of the class struggle, Lenin contributed something new to the general treasury of Marxism as compared with what was created by Marx and Engels, with what could be created

From J. V. Stalin, *Works*, Vol. X, August–December 1927 (Moscow: Foreign Languages Publishing House, 1954), pp. 97–105.

in the pre-imperialist period of capitalism; at the same time Lenin's new contribution to the treasury of Marxism is wholly and completely based on the principles laid down by Marx and Engels.

It is in this sense that we speak of Leninism as Marxism of the era of imperialism and proletarian revolutions.

Here are a few questions to which Lenin contributed something new, developing further the teaching of Marx.

Firstly, the question of monopoly capitalism, of imperialism as the new phase of capitalism.

In *Capital*, Marx and Engels analysed the foundations of capitalism. But Marx and Engels lived in the period of the domination of pre-monopoly capitalism, in the period of the smooth evolution of capitalism and its "peaceful" expansion over the whole world.

That old phase of capitalism came to a close towards the end of the nineteenth and the beginning of the twentieth century, when Marx and Engels were already dead. It is understandable that Marx and Engels could only guess at the new conditions for the development of capitalism that arose as a result of the new phase of capitalism which succeeded the old phase, as a result of the imperialist, monopoly phase of development, when the smooth evolution of capitalism was succeeded by spasmodic, cataclysmic development of capitalism, when the unevenness of development and the contradictions of capitalism became particularly pronounced, and when the struggle for markets and fields of capital export, in the circumstances of the extreme unevenness of development, made periodical imperialist wars for periodic redivisions of the world and of spheres of influence inevitable.

The service Lenin rendered here, and consequently, his new contribution, was that, on the basis of the fundamental principles in *Capital*, he made a substantiated Marxist analysis of imperialism as the last phase of capitalism, and exposed its ulcers and the conditions of its inevitable doom. That analysis formed the basis for Lenin's thesis that under the conditions of imperialism the victory of

socialism is possible in individual capitalist countries, taken separately.

Secondly, the question of the dictatorship of the proletariat.

The fundamental idea of the dictatorship of the proletariat as the political rule of the proletariat and as a method of overthrowing the power of capital by the use of force was advanced by Marx and Engels.

Lenin's new contribution in this field was that:

a) he discovered the Soviet system as the best state form of the dictatorship of the proletariat, utilising for this the experience of the Paris Commune and the Russian revolution;

b) he elucidated the formula of the dictatorship of the proletariat from the angle of the problem of the allies of the proletariat, defining the dictatorship of the proletariat as a special form of class alliance between the proletariat, as the leader, and the exploited masses of the non-proletarian classes (the peasantry, etc.), as the led;

c) he laid particular emphasis on the fact that the dictatorship of the proletariat is the highest type of democracy in class society, the form of *proletarian* democracy, which expresses the interests of the majority (the exploited), in contrast to *capitalist* democracy, which expresses the interests of the minority (the exploiters).

Thirdly, the question of the forms and methods of successfully building socialism in the period of the dictatorship of the proletariat, in the period of transition from capitalism to socialism, in a country surrounded by capitalist states.

Marx and Engels regarded the period of the dictatorship of the proletariat as a more or less prolonged one, full of revolutionary clashes and civil wars, in the course of which the proletariat, being in power, would take the economic, political, cultural and organisational measures necessary for creating, in the place of the old, capitalist society, a new, socialist society, a society without classes and without a state. Lenin wholly and completely based himself on these fundamental principles of Marx and Engels.

Lenin's new contribution in this field was that:

a) he proved that a complete socialist society can be built in the land of the dictatorship of the proletariat surrounded by imperialist states, provided the country is not strangled by the military intervention of the surrounding capitalist states;

b) he traced the concrete lines of economic policy (the "New Economic Policy") by which the proletariat, having possession of the economic key positions (industry, land, transport, banks, etc.), links up socialised industry with agriculture ("the link between industry and peasant economy") and thus leads the whole national economy towards socialism;

c) he traced the concrete ways of gradually guiding and drawing the main mass of the peasantry into the channel of socialist construction through the cooperatives, which in the hands of the proletarian dictatorship are a most powerful instrument for the transformation of small peasant economy and for the re-education of the main mass of the peasantry in the spirit of socialism.

Fourthly, the question of the hegemony of the proletariat in the revolution, in every popular revolution, both in the revolution against tsarism and in the revolution against capitalism.

Marx and Engels provided the main outlines of the idea of the hegemony of the proletariat. Lenin's new contribution in this field was that he further developed and expanded those outlines into a harmonious system of the hegemony of the proletariat, into a harmonious system of leadership of the working masses in town and country by the proletariat not only in the overthrow of tsarism and capitalism, but also in the building of socialism under the dictatorship of the proletariat.

We know that, thanks to Lenin and his Party, the idea of the hegemony of the proletariat was applied in a masterly way in Russia. This, incidentally, explains why the revolution in Russia brought the proletariat into power.

In the past, things usually took the following course: during the revolution the workers fought at the barricades, it was they who shed their blood and overthrew the old order, but power fell into the hands of the bourgeoisie, who then oppressed and exploited the workers. That was the case in England and France. That was the case in Germany. Here, in Russia, however, things took a different turn. In Russia the workers were not merely the shock force of the revolution. While being the shock force of the revolution, the Russian proletariat at the same time strove for hegemony, for political leadership of all the exploited masses of town and country, rallying them around itself, wresting them from the bourgeoisie and politically isolating the bourgeoisie. And while being the leader of the exploited masses, the Russian proletariat fought to take power into its own hands and to utilise it in its own interests, against the bourgeoisie, against capitalism. This, in fact, explains why each powerful outbreak of the revolution in Russia, in October 1905 as well as in February 1917, brought on to the scene Soviets of Workers' Deputies as the embryo of the new apparatus of power whose function is to suppress the bourgeoisie—as against the bourgeois parliament, the old apparatus of power, whose function is to suppress the proletariat.

Twice the bourgeoisie in Russia tried to restore the bourgeois parliament and put an end to the Soviets: in September 1917, at the time of the Pre-parliament, before the seizure of power by the Bolsheviks, and in January 1918, at the time of the Constituent Assembly, after the seizure of power by the proletariat; and on both occasions it suffered defeat. Why? Because the bourgeoisie was already politically isolated, because the vast masses of the working people regarded the proletariat as the sole leader of the revolution, and because the Soviets had already been tried and tested by the masses as their own workers' government, to exchange which for a bourgeois parliament would have meant suicide for the proletariat. It is not surprising, therefore, that bourgeois parliamentarism did not take root in Russia. That is why the revolution in Russia led to the rule of the proletariat.

Such were the results of the application of Lenin's system of the hegemony of the proletariat in the revolution.

Fifthly, the national and colonial question.

Analysing in their time the events in Ireland, India, China, the Central European countries, Poland and Hungary, Marx and Engels provided the basic, initial ideas on the national and colonial question. Lenin in his works based himself on those ideas.

Lenin's new contribution in this field was:

a) he unified those ideas in one harmonious system of views on national and colonial revolutions in the era of imperialism;

b) he linked the national and colonial question with the question of overthrowing imperialism;

c) he declared the national and colonial question to be a component part of the general question of international proletarian revolution.

Lastly, the question of the party of the proletariat.

Marx and Engels provided the main outlines on the party as the advanced detachment of the proletariat, without which (the party) the proletariat cannot achieve its emancipation, either in the sense of capturing power, or in the sense of transforming capitalist society.

Lenin's new contribution in this field was that he developed those outlines further in conformity with the new conditions of the struggle of the proletariat in the period of imperialism and showed that:

a) the party is the highest form of class organisation of the proletariat as compared with other forms of proletarian organisation (trade unions, co-operatives, state organisation) whose work it is the party's function to generalise and direct;

b) the dictatorship of the proletariat can be implemented only through the party, as the guiding force of the dictatorship;

c) the dictatorship of the proletariat can be complete only if it is led by one party, the Communist Party, which does not and must not share the leadership with other parties;

d) unless there is iron discipline in the party, the tasks of the dictatorship of the proletariat in regard to suppressing the exploiters and transforming class society into socialist society cannot be accomplished.

That, in the main, is the new contribution made by Lenin in his works, giving concrete form to Marx's teaching and developing it further in conformity with the new conditions of the struggle of the proletariat in the period of imperialism.

That is why we say that Leninism is Marxism of the era of imperialism and proletarian revolutions.

It is clear from this that Leninism cannot be separated from Marxism; still less can it be counterposed to Marxism.

The question submitted by the delegation goes on to say:

"Would it be correct to say that Lenin believed in 'creative revolution' whereas Marx was more inclined to wait for the culmination of the development of economic forces?"

I think it would be quite incorrect to say that. I think that every popular revolution, if it really is a popular revolution, is a creative revolution, for it breaks up the old order and creates a new one.

Of course, there is nothing creative in the "revolutions"—if they may be so called—that sometimes take place in certain backward countries, in the form of toy-like "risings" of one tribe against another. But Marxists never regarded such toy-like "risings" as revolutions. It is obviously not a question of such "risings," but of a mass, popular revolution in which the oppressed classes rise up against the oppressing classes. Such a revolution cannot but be creative. Marx and Lenin upheld precisely such a revolution, and only such a revolution. It goes without saying that such a revolution cannot arise under all conditions, that it can take place only under definite favourable conditions of an economic and political nature.

Nikolai Bukharin

PRACTICAL THEORETICIAN

Lenin's testament described Nikolai Bukharin as the Bolshevik party's foremost theoretician as well as its personally most beloved member. The same document also made the point that the ultra-scholarly nature of Bukharin's views detracted from their value in the political arena. Bukharin, for his part, worshipped Lenin, whom he regarded as his "teacher in revolution." Despite occasional sharp clashes between the two men, Bukharin's respect for his master's intuitive brilliance increased to the day of Lenin's death. The following passage reflects the theoretician's admiration for Lenin's ability to cast theory aside when necessary and to replace it with a program for action that fitted the needs of the moment.

ONE of the most characteristic features of Vladimir Ilyitch,* one of the most curious, was his *realisation of the practical sense of every theoretical construction and of any kind of theoretical conception.* I know it often happened that we even used to joke sometimes amongst ourselves at Vladimir Ilyitch's over-practical attitude towards quite a number of theoretical problems, but, comrades, now when we have already become tempered on the revolutionary anvil after many years, and when we have been able to see and experience a great deal, it seems to me that our merriment should be turned against ourselves, because here again it was nothing more or less than an example of that very same habit of ours, the habit of intellectuals, of definitely narrow specialists, journalists, writers, or people more or less engaged in theory as their special profession. In exactly the same way as Vladimir Ilyitch disliked any kind of verbal acrobatics and specific erudition . . ., he could not bear anything superfluous and approached theoretical conceptions and doctrines in a purely practical manner. Have they any other meaning be-

* Lenin's first name and patronymic. [Editor's note.]

sides the practical one? From the point of view of Marxism, it is clear that they have no other meaning whatsoever. But in so far as we had up to a certain degree been specialists, this damped our ardour and in this respect Lenin saw into the future to a much greater degree than any of us sinners, since what for him was organically disgusting, had for us a certain attractive force. And I think that this well-thought-out realisation, this realisation of the serviceable role of any theoretical construction, no matter how high it might be, constitutes an extraordinarily valuable and positive feature of Leninist Marxism.

There is another curious feature connected with this, which could never be understood without the first. This feature might be termed "de-fetishisation," or, in other words, the expulsion of any fetish-like cliché or dogma from any position, etc. At first, we were very often astonished at the unusual audacity with which Vladimir Ilyitch tackled certain theoretical or practical problems. Remember such incidents as the Brest-Litovsk peace, when Vladimir Ilyitch raised the question as to whether one might take arms from one foreign power

From Nikolai Bukharin, *Lenin as a Marxist* (London: The Communist Party of Great Britain, 1925), pp. 28–33, 40–49.

for use against the other; this troubled our international conscience to its very depths. Meanwhile, our "international-ism" was lulled by the theoretical igno-rance as to the fact that when we took over power the whole landscape changed. Remember the slogan "Learn to trade," which offended the eye of many a good revolutionary and also had a theoretical substratum and which con-nected with quite a number of theoreti-cal conceptions. The only person capa-ble of such theoretical audacity, together with this practice is a person, an ideolo-gist, a theoretician and practician who himself wields the exceedingly sharp weapon of Marxism, but who, at the same time, never understood Marxism as some sort of lukewarm dogma, but as an instrument for orientation in definite surroundings, a man who thoroughly understood that every new external cor-relation should inevitably be followed by some other reaction of conduct on the part of the workers' Party and the work-ing class. Indeed, just see how Vladimir Ilyitch formulated this conception in general. I do not wish to burden you with quotations and have not brought any ex-tracts with me, nor have I even worked on any; but I will remind you of a series of points and formulae which Vladimir Ilyitch presented. One of his most com-mon tactical formulae concerning expe-rience, reads:

A very great many errors occur through slogans and measures, which were quite correct in a definite historical phase and in a definite state of affairs, being mechani-cally transferred to another historical set-ting, other correlation of forces and to other situations.

That is one of the general tactical for-mulae. Let us examine the ideology of our opponents, let us take such a prob-lem as democracy for instance. We also were all democrats during a definite pe-riod, we all demanded the democratic re-public and the Constituent Assembly, only a few months before we overthrew it. That is quite natural. But, neverthe-less, only those who understood the rela-tive social role of these slogans, who un-derstood that under the capitalist regime

we cannot present demands to the capi-talists, could adopt any other orienta-tion. And, for this reason, freedom for our workers' organisations had inevi-tably to receive the formula: "Freedom for all." When we pass into another his-torical phase and situation, we must abandon this formula. Those who ad-hered to and made a fetish of it, did not keep up with the march of events and were to be found on the other side of the barricade. This is but a minor example, but there is an endless quantity of such instances. Vladimir Ilyitch stood out as having astonishing audacity in this re-spect.

Let us now take another question in its general formulation. I spoke here about the evolutionary aspect *after* we had carried through the revolution. Take for instance such slogans of Lenin's as "Learn to trade," or "One specialist is better than such and such a number of Communists." The practical sense of these slogans is now clear to us. They were quite correct but, in order to be able to say these things, it is quite evident that some theoretical thinking was nec-essary. In so far as the situation has changed, one must act in quite another manner. At the present time the correla-tion between the ideology of our Commu-nists, and on the other hand the neces-sity to attract non-Communists, is of such a nature that it was necessary here to carry out quite a new and peculiar pol-icy of a *constructive* nature. If in former times such words as "tradesmen," "trade," "bank," and so forth sounded like words of insult for any revolution-ary, now, in order to pass on to the slo-gan "Learn to trade," the most profound thinking was essential on a number of theoretical basic questions of great im-portance in principle. What for us is *only* now just a self-evident thing, was thought out theoretically by Lenin down to the most minor detail. After all it is only the vulgar superficial consciousness of our opponents that represents Vladi-mir Ilyitch as a man hewn out with an axe, something after the fashion of a statuette from the time of the Stone Age. As a matter of fact, this is absolutely un-true. If comrade Lenin launched some simple slogans such as "Rob the robbers," this sounded unusually terrible and barbaric for all our civilised opponents; whereas, as a matter of fact, this was but a result of profound theoretical thinking as to what slogan must now be issued, as to what is the mass psychology at the present moment, and as to what the masses will understand and will not understand.

Lenin always approached the question in such a way as to obtain alliance with the greatest possible number of the people who could play the role of known quantities of energy to hurl against the old regime. This demanded very elaborate theoretical thinking. But when Lenin said "It is necessary to learn to trade," this sounded very paradoxical, although now that appears to us quite evident. Every serious step that Vladimir Ilyitch took, both in the theoretical and in the practical field, was in its own way a placing in position of Columbus' egg. When Columbus' egg was put in position it appeared to everyone that it could only be made to stand up in that manner. And here you have this slogan "Learn to trade," which is dependent upon a number of theoretical calculations and solutions of theoretical problems, the problem of correlation between town and village, the problem of the role of the currency process—in general the problem as to the role of the trading apparatus in this currency process. This was not merely a slogan taken down from the shelf, it was simply a practical watchword formulation of quite a number of theoretical conceptions which had been thought out step by step. Only when you begin to read the thoughts of Vladimir Ilyitch volume by volume, and combine the definite sectors of his thinking, will you be presented with a clear picture of the ideological path which Vladimir Ilyitch trod when working out these problems. Lenin was only able to carry out all these big moves so successfully as a strategist, because he was a very strong theorist who was able quite clearly to analyse the given combination of class forces, take proper stock of them, make theoretical generalisations and from these theoretical generalisations draw the corresponding practical-political conclusions. What lay at the bottom of all this was the fact that Lenin wielded the Marxist weapon in a masterly way. Lenin never allowed it to get cool or to remain motionless. It was always a really powerful instrument which, in Lenin's hands, was turned round to one side or to the other according to the demands of *practical actuality*. It was the Marxism which, vulgarly speaking, has nothing sacred except the interests of the social revolution. It is an ideological instrument of such a time that knows no fetishes whatsoever, and which understands to a nicety the significance of any theoretical doctrine, of any move, of any separate theoretical conception, that is foreign to anything lukewarm.

How did Vladimir Ilyitch approach a number of problems? When within the Party or outside its ranks there arose among us some kind of theoretical digression from Marxism, he at once approached this with a definite practical gauge, because he bound up theory with practice so excellently and excellently deciphered any verbal superficiality. I said above that if Marx possessed the algebra of capitalist development and the algebra of revolution, Lenin had both the algebra of a new period, and, I repeat, the arithmetic.

*   *   *

In proceeding further, it is important that we should approach the question of *the working class and the peasantry*. I need not enlarge upon the role which this problem plays in our practical politics. But the further we proceed with the development of the revolution in other countries, the more we see that this problem has not only a Russian significance but that this problem has also an enormous significance for quite a number of other countries, and one might say that these countries, in which this problem has not a great significance, are exceptions to the rule. One could count on one's fingers those countries where the peasant problem, combined with the problem of the revolution, does not play the most outstanding role. Of course, the basis for the solution of this problem was laid in the general Marxist theory and it goes without saying that the methodics of the solution of this question are also contained in the general Marxist conception. We all know Marx's formulae with regard to Germany in which he talks about the desired happy combination of forces from the point of view of the victorious workers' revolution, when the proletarian revolution should coincide with a peasant war. Marx foresaw the most favourable events from the point of view of the development of a victorious workers' revolution. But the special working out of this problem, which from the viewpoint of the strategy and tactics of the class struggle is a primary problem, is the work of Lenin alone. Of course, much may be explained here by the fact that Vladimir Ilyitch was born, grew up and acted above all in a country where in view of its social-economic structure the peasant problem could not but attract great attention. But bear in mind that here it was not just a question of asserting this fact, but of an actual exceedingly extensive working out of this problem, starting from the most fundamental, deep theoretical problems and ending with practical-political conclusions.

It seems to me that Vladimir Ilyitch was the most outstanding *agrarian theoretician* existing among Marxists. In his works the agrarian problem is the question to which the best pages were devoted. From the very beginning of his conscious activities as an economist and statistician, Vladimir Ilyitch began to take up the agrarian problem and a number of problems of a more abstract nature, such as that of "diminishing fertility of the soil," that of absolute rent, etc., ending with questions of a practical nature, all bearing on the relations between the working class and the peasantry. All these problems were worked out and developed by Vladimir Ilyitch in the most detailed fashion. I do not believe anyone did so much, so much that was essentially important in the field of the agrarian problem, as Vladimir Ilyitch did. Furthermore, if we had been faced with another degree of abstraction, we

might then restrict ourselves to analyses of abstract capitalist society where such remnants of feudal relations, such as the peasantry, play no essential role and may be discarded from the analysis. But no sooner is it a question of commencing to decipher algebraic formulae and transforming them into arithmetical formulae or into formulae of a certain category that one might reasonably represent as occupying a certain intermediate position between algebra and arithmetic, then you at once begin to get down to this question.

The recognition of the fact that the working class must have on its side during the period of the Socialist revolution some ally as representative of the great mass of the people, led to the analysis of the agrarian question. And Lenin's teachings of the alliance of the working class and the peasantry and the relations between these two classes is one of the corner-stones of all that is specific in Vladimir Ilyitch's additions to the general Marxist teaching.

At this point it is interesting to remark that this teaching was developed in the struggle on two fronts: on the one hand it developed in the struggle against the Narodniki, and on the other hand it developed in the struggle against specifically liberal Marxism, if one may say so. Vladimir Ilyitch fought on these two fronts both theoretically and practically, and, from the political point of view and from the viewpoint of revolutionary practice, this struggle is quite adequately and clearly explained in the fact that it was the problem of an ally of the working class that was being solved; for the working class, aiming at the victorious development of the Socialist revolution, this problem was connected with yet another deep-rooted problem which had to be acknowledged both theoretically and practically—this was the problem of the *hegemony of the proletariat*. It was necessary to explore theoretically such a position as would make it possible to liberate the peasantry from the influence of the liberals, and of any other bourgeois influence, and unite them with the working class: the most serious practical problem which distinguished us from the Mensheviks and S.R.'s was whether the working class should ally itself with the liberal bourgeoisie or should the working class go with the peasantry or should the peasantry stand above all other groupings. The radical Narodniki group always placed the peasantry first. The liberal Narodniki stood for an alliance with the liberal bourgeoisie, which was to have the hegemony over the peasantry. The Menshevik formula was for the support of the liberal bourgeoisie by the working class.

It is natural that from all these combinations the only correct one was a combination of the working class with the peasantry, in such a form as would allow the working class to lead the peasantry. This was the practical background for a number of theoretical problems. From this aspect, Lenin examined all problems under the common heading "The Agrarian Question," in its entirety, in its extensive historical scale, and in all its details and subsidiary problems arising therefrom. In this respect we must also remark that in the future this problem is still bound to play a colossal role. This is because, whereas, on one side it is bound up with the problem of the hegemony of the proletariat, on the other side it is connected with the national and colonial questions.

If we raise ourselves above our present planet and survey the whole extent of the game from an international scale, if we survey the whole of Europe as an entity, if we review the industrial parts of America, if we compare the whole of Western Europe with all the colonies, with China, with India and with the other colonial dependencies, we will then quite clearly perceive that the national revolutionary movement and the colonial movement, or rather the combination of these two, represent but another form of the problem of the relations of the working class and the peasantry. For if Western Europe, taken in the general setting of world economy, represents a great collective town, the colonial dependencies of the capitalist countries represent a huge village. And in so far as the industrial proletariat of the industrial countries enters the arena uniting its forces for an attack on the capitalist regime, in so far as this proletariat leads into the fight millions and yet more millions of colonial slaves, for these reasons these slaves are nothing more or less than the great peasant reserve of the international revolution. Therefore, the problem as to the relations of the working class with the peasantry thus leads to still another problem to which I have already made allusion— that of nationals, national wars and colonial risings.

This problem, comrades, has thus still to play an important role. Here, also, the first fundamental words were spoken by the Lenin school. The development of this problem, the corner-stones of the theoretical conception and the basic line observable here have been undoubtedly given by Vladimir Ilyitch.

Klara Zetkin

DESPISER OF BOURGEOIS MORALS

In 1900 German Socialist Klara Zetkin helped to smuggle the first issue of *Iskra* from Germany into Russia. She first saw Lenin in 1907 at the World Congress of the Second International at Stuttgart, where Rosa Luxemburg pointed him out to her as a man who would "try to overturn mountains." In 1915 Zetkin joined Luxemburg and Liebknecht and others in forming the Spartacus League, a radical offshoot from the German Socialist Party, and supported Lenin's anti-war stand at the Zimmerwald Conference. Subsequently, Zetkin organized and led the international women's communist movement and helped found the German Communist Party. She idolized Lenin, and much of her political activity was guided by his views. In this excerpt Zetkin reveals the great extent to which Marxism influenced Lenin's thinking about the place of women and of sex in modern society.

COMRADE Lenin repeatedly discussed with me the problem of women's rights. Needless to say he saw full social equality of women as a principle which no Communist could dispute.

We had our first lengthy talk on this subject in the autumn of 1920, in Lenin's big study in the Kremlin.

Speaking of conditions among women in the German Communist Party, Lenin said:

"I have heard strange things about German comrades. I understand that in Hamburg a gifted Communist woman is bringing out a newspaper for prostitutes, and is trying to organise them for the revolutionary struggle. Now Rosa [Luxemburg], a true Communist, acted like a human being when she wrote an article in defence of prostitutes who have landed in jail for violating a police regulation concerning their sad trade. They are double victims of bourgeois society. Victims, first, of its accursed system of property and, secondly, of its accursed moral hypocrisy. There's no doubt about this. Only a coarse-grained and short-sighted person could forget this. To understand this is one thing, but it is quite another thing—how shall I put it?—to organise the prostitutes as a special revolutionary guild contingent and publish a trade union paper for them. Are there really no industrial working women left in Germany who need organising, who need a newspaper, who should be enlisted in your struggle? This is a morbid deviation. It strongly reminds me of the literary vogue which made a sweet madonna out of every prostitute. Its origin was sound too: social sympathy, and indignation against the moral hypocrisy of the honourable bourgeoisie. But the healthy principle underwent bourgeois corrosion and degenerated. The question of prostitution will confront us even in our country with many a difficult problem. Return the prostitute to productive work, find her a place in the social economy—that is the thing to do. But the present state of our economy and all the other circumstances make it a difficult and complicated matter. Here you have an aspect of the woman problem which faces us in all its magnitude, after the proletariat has come to power, and demands a practical solution. It will still require a great deal of effort here in So-

From V. I. Lenin, *On the Emancipation of Women* (Moscow: Progress Publishers, n.d.), pp. 93–104. Adapted and abridged.

viet Russia. But to return to your special problem in Germany. Under no circumstances should the Party look calmly upon such improper acts of its members. It causes confusion and splits our forces. Now what have *you* done to stop it?"

Before I could answer Lenin continued:

"The record of your sins, Klara, is even worse. I have been told that at the evenings arranged for reading and discussion with working women, sex and marriage problems come first. They are said to be the main objects of interest in your political instruction and educational work. I could not believe my ears when I heard that. The first state of proletarian dictatorship is battling with the counter-revolutionaries of the whole world. The situation in Germany itself calls for the greatest unity of all proletarian revolutionary forces, so that they can repel the counter-revolution which is pushing on. But active Communist women are busy discussing sex problems and the forms of marriage—'past, present and future. They consider it their most important task to enlighten working women on these questions. It is said that a pamphlet on the sex question written by a Communist authoress from Vienna enjoys the greatest popularity. What rot that booklet is! The workers read what is right in it long ago in Bebel. Only not in the tedious, cut-and-dried form found in the pamphlet but in the form of gripping agitation that strikes out at bourgeois society. The mention of Freud's hypotheses is designed to give the pamphlet a scientific veneer, but it is so much bungling by an amateur. Freud's theory has now become a fad. I mistrust sex theories expounded in articles, treatises, pamphlets, etc.—in short, the theories dealt with in that specific literature which sprouts so luxuriantly on the dung heap of bourgeois society. I mistrust those who are always absorbed in the sex problems, the way an Indian saint is absorbed in the contemplation of his navel. It seems to me that this superabundance of sex theories, which for the most part are mere hypotheses, and often quite arbitrary ones, stems from a personal need. It springs from the desire

to justify one's own abnormal or excessive sex life before bourgeois morality and to plead for tolerance towards oneself. This veiled respect for bourgeois morality is as repugnant to me as rooting about in all that bears on sex. No matter how rebellious and revolutionary it may be made to appear, it is in the final analysis thoroughly bourgeois. Intellectuals and others like them are particularly keen on this. There is no room for it in the Party, among the class-conscious, fighting proletariat."

I interposed that where private property and the bourgeois social order prevail, questions of sex and marriage gave rise to manifold problems, conflicts and suffering for women of all social classes and strata. As far as women are concerned, the war and its consequences exacerbated the existing conflicts and suffering to the utmost precisely in the sphere of sexual relations. Problems formerly concealed from women were now laid bare. To this was added the atmosphere of incipient revolution. The world of old emotions and thoughts was cracking up. Former social connections were loosening and breaking. The makings of new relations between people were appearing. Interest in the relevant problems was an expression of the need for enlightenment and a new orientation. It was also a reaction against the distortions and hypocrisy of bourgeois society. Knowledge of the modifications of the forms of marriage and family that took place in the course of history, and of their dependence on economics, would serve to rid the minds of working women of their preconceived idea of the eternity of bourgeois society. The critically historical attitude to this had to lead to an unrelenting analysis of bourgeois society, an exposure of its essence and its consequences, including the branding of false sex morality. All roads led to Rome. Every truly Marxist analysis of an important part of the ideological superstructure of society, of an outstanding social phenomenon, had to lead to an analysis of bourgeois society and its foundation, private property. It should lead to the conclusion that "Carthage must be destroyed."

Lenin nodded with a smile.

"There you are! You defend your comrades and your Party like a lawyer. What you say is of course true. But that can at best excuse, not justify, the mistake made in Germany. It remains a mistake. Can you assure me in all sincerity that during those reading and discussion evenings, questions of sex and marriage are dealt with from the point of view of mature, vital historical materialism? This presupposes wide-ranging, profound knowledge, and the fullest Marxist mastery of a vast amount of material. Do you now have the forces you need for that? Had you had them, a pamphlet like the one we spoke about would not have been used for instruction during reading and discussion evenings. It is being recommended and disseminated instead of being criticised. Why is the approach to this problem inadequate and un-Marxist? Because sex and marriage problems are not treated as only part of the main social problem. Conversely, the main social problem is presented as a part, an appendage to the sex problem. The important point recedes .into the background. Thus not only is this question obscured, but also thought, and the class-consciousness of working women in general, is dulled.

"Besides, and this isn't the least important point, Solomon the Wise said there is a time for everything. I ask you, is this the time to keep working women busy for months at a stretch with such questions as how to love or be loved, how to woo or be wooed? This, of course, with regard to the 'past, present and future,' and among the various races. Nowadays all the thoughts of Communist women, of working women, should be centred on the proletarian revolution, which will lay the foundation, among other things, for the necessary revision of marital and sexual relations. Just now we must really give priority to problems other than the forms of marriage prevalent among Australia's aborigines, or marriage between brother and sister in ancient times. For the German proletariat, the problem of the Soviets, of the Versailles Treaty and its impact on the lives of women, the problem of unem-ployment, of falling wages, of taxes and many other things remain the order of the day. To be brief, I am still of the opinion that this sort of political and social education of working women is wrong, absolutely wrong. How could you keep quiet about it? You should have set your authority against it."

I told my fervent friend that I had never failed to criticise and to remonstrate with the leading women comrades in various places. But, as he knew, no prophet is honoured in his own country or in his own house. By my criticism I had drawn upon myself the suspicion that "survivals of a Social-Democratic attitude and old-fashioned philistinism were still strong" in my mind. However, in the end my criticism had proved effective. Sex and marriage were no longer the focal point in lectures at discussion evenings. Lenin resumed the thread of his argument.

"Yes, yes, I know that," he said. "Many people rather suspect *me* of philistinism on this account, although such an attitude is repugnant to me—it conceals so much narrowmindedness and hypocrisy. Well, I'm unruffled by it. Yellow-beaked fledgelings newly hatched from their bourgeois-tainted eggs are all so terribly clever. We have to put up with that without mending our ways. The youth movement is also affected with the modern approach to the sex problem and with excessive interest in it."

Lenin emphasised the word "modern" with an ironical, deprecating gesture.

"I was also told that sex problems are a favourite subject in your youth organisations too, and that there are hardly enough lecturers on this subject. This nonsense is especially dangerous and damaging to the youth movement. It can easily lead to sexual excesses, to over-stimulation of sex life and to wasted health and strength of young people. You must fight that too. There is no lack of contact between the youth movement and the women's movement. Our Communist women everywhere should co-operate methodically with young people. This will be a continuation of motherhood, will elevate it and extend it from the individual to the social sphere.

Women's incipient social life and activities must be promoted, so that they can outgrow the narrowness of their philistine, individualistic psychology centred on home and family. But this is incidental.

"In our country, too, considerable numbers of young people are busy 'revising bourgeois conceptions and morals' in the sex question. And let me add that this involves a considerable section of our best boys and girls, of our truly promising youth. It is as you have just said. In the atmosphere created by the aftermath of war and by the revolution which has begun, old ideological values, finding themselves in a society whose economic foundations are undergoing a radical change, perish, and lose their restraining force. New values crystallise slowly, in the struggle. With regard to relations between people, and between man and woman, feelings and thoughts are also becoming revolutionised. New boundaries are being drawn between the rights of the individual and those of the community, and hence also the duties of the individual. Things are still in complete, chaotic ferment. The direction and potentiality of the various contradictory tendencies can still not be seen clearly enough. It is a slow and often very painful process of passing away and coming into being. All this applies also to the field of sexual relations, marriage, and the family. The decay, putrescence, and filth of bourgeois marriage with its difficult dissolution, its licence for the husband and bondage for the wife, and its disgustingly false sex morality and relations fill the best and most spiritually active of people with the utmost loathing.

"The coercion of bourgeois marriage and bourgeois legislation on the family enhance the evil and aggravate the conflicts. It is the coercion of 'sacrosanct' property. It sanctifies venality, baseness, and dirt. The conventional hypocrisy of 'respectable' bourgeois society takes care of the rest. People revolt against the prevailing abominations and perversions. And at a time when mighty nations are being destroyed, when the former power relations are being disrupted, when a whole social world is beginning to decline, the sensations of the individual undergo a rapid change. A stimulating thirst for different forms of enjoyment easily acquires an irresistible force. Sexual and marriage reforms in the bourgeois sense will not do. In the sphere of sexual relations and marriage, a revolution is approaching—in keeping with the proletarian revolution. Of course, women and young people are taking a deep interest in the complex tangle of problems which have arisen as a result of this. Both the former and the latter suffer greatly from the present messy state of sex relations. Young people rebel against them with the vehemence of their years. This is only natural. Nothing could be falser than to preach monastic self-denial and the sanctity of the filthy bourgeois morals to young people. However, it is hardly a good thing that sex, already strongly felt in the physical sense, should at such a time assume so much prominence in the psychology of young people. The consequences are nothing short of fatal.

"Youth's altered attitude to questions of sex is of course 'fundamental,' and based on theory. Many people call it 'revolutionary' and 'communist.' They sincerely believe that this is so. I am an old man, and I do not like it. I may be a morose ascetic, but quite often this so-called 'new sex life' of young people—and frequently of the adults too—seems to me purely bourgeois and simply an extension of the good old bourgeois brothel. All this has nothing in common with free love as we Communists understand it. No doubt you have heard about the famous theory that in communist society satisfying sexual desire and the craving for love is as simple and trivial as 'drinking a glass of water.' A section of our youth has gone mad, absolutely mad, over this 'glass-of-water theory.' It has been fatal to many a young boy and girl. Its devotees assert that it is a Marxist theory. I want no part of the kind of Marxism which infers all phenomena and all changes in the ideological superstructure of society directly and blandly from its economic basis, for things are not as simple as all that. A certain Frederick Engels has established this a long time ago with regard to historical materialism.

"I consider the famous 'glass-of-water' theory as completely un-Marxist and, moreover, as anti-social. It is not only what nature has given but also what has become culture, whether of a high or low level, that comes into play in sexual life. Engels pointed out in his *Origin of the Family* how significant it was that the common sexual relations had developed into individual sex love and thus became purer. The relations between the sexes are not simply the expression of a mutual influence between economics and a physical want deliberately singled out for physiological examination. It would be rationalism and not Marxism to attempt to refer the change in these relations directly to the economic basis of society in isolation from its connection with the ideology as a whole. To be sure, thirst has to be quenched. But would a normal person normally lie down in the gutter and drink from a puddle? Or even from a glass whose edge has been greased by many lips? But the social aspect is more important than anything else. The drinking of water is really an individual matter. But it takes two people to make love, and a third person, a new life, is likely to come into being. This deed has a social complexion and constitutes a duty to the community.

"As a Communist I have no liking at all for the 'glass-of-water' theory, despite its attractive label: 'emancipation of love.' Besides, emancipation of love is neither a novel nor a communistic idea. You will recall that it was advanced in fine literature around the middle of the past century as 'emancipation of the heart.' In bourgeois practice it materialised into emancipation of the flesh. It was preached with greater talent than now, though I cannot judge how it was practised. Not that I want my criticism to breed asceticism. That is farthest from my thoughts. Communism should not bring asceticism, but joy and strength, stemming, among other things, from a consummate love life. Whereas today, in my opinion, the obtaining plethora of sex life yields neither joy nor strength. On the contrary, it impairs them. This is bad, very bad, indeed, in the epoch of revolution.

"Young people are particularly in need of joy and strength. Healthy sports, such as gymnastics, swimming, hiking, physical exercises of every description and a wide range of intellectual interests is what they need, as well as learning, study and research, and as far as possible collectively. This will be far more useful to young people than endless lectures and discussions on sex problems and the so-called living by one's nature. *Mens sana in corpore sano*. Be neither monk nor Don Juan, but not anything in between either, like a German philistine. You know the young comrade X. He is a splendid lad, and highly gifted. For all that, I am afraid that he will never amount to anything. He has one love affair after another. This is not good for the political struggle and for the revolution. I will not vouch for the reliability or the endurance of women whose love affair is intertwined with politics, or for the men who run after every petticoat and let themselves in with every young female. No, no, that does not go well with revolution."

Lenin sprang to his feet, slapped the table with his hand and paced up and down the room.

"The revolution calls for concentration and rallying of every nerve by the masses and by the individual. It does not tolerate orgiastic conditions so common among d'Annunzio's decadent heroes and heroines. Promiscuity in sexual matters is bourgeois. It is a sign of degeneration. The proletariat is a rising class. It does not need an intoxicant to stupefy or stimulate it, neither the intoxicant of sexual laxity or of alcohol. It should and will not forget the vileness, the filth and the barbarity of capitalism. It derives its strongest inspiration to fight from its class position, from the communist ideal. What it needs is clarity, clarity, and more clarity. Therefore, I repeat, there must be no weakening, no waste and no dissipation of energy. Self-control and self-discipline are not slavery; not in matters of love either. But excuse me, Klara, I have strayed far from the point which we set out to discuss. Why have you not called me to order? Worry has set me talking. I take the future of our youth very close to heart. It is part and parcel of the revolution. Whenever harmful elements appear, which creep from bourgeois society to the world of the revolution and spread like the roots of prolific weeds, it is better to take action against them quickly. The questions we have dealt with are also part of the women's problems."

I. Korotkov

DIAGNOSTICIAN OF COLD WAR

Colonel Korotkov is an officer in the Soviet Army and a contributor to Soviet military journals. His article, appearing in an official Soviet publication, inescapably reflects the propaganda line of its day. Nevertheless, it is well worth reading for its comprehensive summary of Lenin's Marxian views on war—war as shaped by history's all-pervasive class struggle. Lenin's distinction between just and unjust wars, it might be added, provides convenient ideological support for whatever military or diplomatic position the Soviet Union might choose to adopt at any given moment.

AT the close of the nineteenth century the centre of the revolutionary movement in Europe shifted to Russia, and the cardinal practical task of the Russian Marxists became to prepare for the proletarian revolution. At a time when the entire system of imperialism had matured for a socialist revolution Lenin comprehensively analysed, from the dialectical-materialistic viewpoint, the problem of force and, in particular, its most extreme and critical form—war between opposing classes and between states and nations. He repeatedly emphasised that the exploiting classes ruled mainly with the aid of armed forces; the working class and the working masses generally had therefore to be prepared and able to oppose them in order to defend their interests and paralyse the ability of the oppressors to use force. In *Revolutionary Army and Revolutionary Government*, written in 1905, he pointed out that no Marxist had ever doubted the tremendous importance of military knowledge, of military technique, and of military organisation as an instrument which the masses of the people, and classes of the people, use in resolving great historical conflicts.

From the reminiscences of Lenin's associates we know how assiduously he studied the works of military theoreti-cians of the past and present. In his library in the Kremlin there are some 200 books on military problems by bourgeois and Soviet authors. He was particularly interested in the combat experience of the Paris Commune (1871), the Russo-Japanese War (1904–05), the First Russian Revolution (1905–1907) and the First World War (1914–18). His numerous works and speeches on war and armies contain important theoretical propositions that have retained their significance to this day.*

As the leader of the Communist Party, Lenin was interested in both general and specific problems of war. A scientific analysis showed Marxists that war was a socio-political phenomenon that came into being with the transition from classless, primitive communal system to exploiter society split up into hostile classes. Consequently, by bringing to light the political relations between classes, states and nations it is possible to lay bare the essence of war. War, Lenin explained, is a continuation of

* Lenin's speeches on military problems have been published in two editions in the USSR in the series *Officers' Library: Lenin on War, Armies and Military Science* in two volumes (1957), *Lenin on War, Armies and Military Science* (1965): and also V. I. Lenin, *Military Correspondence* (1917–22)—first edition in 1956, and second edition in 1966.

From I. Korotkov, "The Military-Theoretical Legacy of Lenin," *Soviet Military Review*, April 1968, pp. 2–6.

politics, and in order to understand war one must correctly understand politics, which boil down to relations between classes. If it was an imperialist policy, Lenin said, i.e., one designed to safeguard the interests of finance capital and rob and oppress colonies and foreign countries, then the war stemming from that policy was imperialist. If it was a national-liberation policy, i.e., one expressive of the mass movement against national oppression, then the war stemming from that policy was a war of national liberation.

In *The Collapse of the Second International* (1915), Lenin wrote: "With reference to wars, the main thesis of dialectics . . . is that *'war is simply the continuation of politics by other* (i.e., violent) *means . . .'* And it was always the standpoint of Marx and Engels, who regarded *any* war as the *continuation* of the politics of the powers concerned— and the *various classes* within these countries—in a definite period." This thesis lucidly gives the inner foundation, nature and essence of all wars without exception.

Wars, Lenin said, have always been a weapon, a continuation of politics because every war is prepared and started for political, class considerations and acquires a political character. Therefore, first it is necessary to elucidate the question of what classes fought a given war and the aims they pursued, "what classes staged and directed it."

Lenin never failed to make the point that politics are incomparably more complex than war, which is their component, a destructive means that always brings suffering to the people. As a continuation of politics, war is a dual process in which one adversary fights to preserve and strengthen existing political relations and the other to destroy these relations or fundamentally change them. No war can be correctly understood without an understanding of the nature of the political relations between the belligerents.

A Caricature of Marxism and Imperialist Economism, which Lenin wrote in 1916, contains the following words: "Marxism . . . says: if the 'substance' of a war is, *for example*, the overthrow of alien oppression . . . then such a war is progressive as far as the oppressed state or nation is concerned. *If*, however, the 'substance' of a war is redivision of colonies, division of booty, plunder of foreign lands (and such is the war of 1914–16), then all talk of defending the fatherland is 'sheer deception of the people.' "

Lenin pointed out that by their political substance wars can be divided into "just and unjust, progressive and reactionary wars, wars of the progressive classes and wars of the backward classes, wars serving to increase class oppression, and wars serving to overthrow this oppression."

Wars are unjust when they are a continuation of anti-popular policies and are fought to further the mercenary interests of the exploiters, to preserve, extend or restore their reactionary rule over the working class, the working masses, and peoples of colonies or less developed and dependent countries. They are· a means by which the ruling exploiting classes enrich themselves, and seize foreign territories, markets and sources of raw material.

Just wars are the antipode to unjust wars. These are civil wars of the working class against the bourgeoisie; wars in defence of socialist states against imperialist aggressors; national-liberation wars of the peoples of colonies and dependent countries against the colonial system of imperialism; liberation wars for national and state sovereignty by the peoples of bourgeois countries attacked by imperialist invaders.

By the example of many military conflicts, Lenin showed that there are wars in which both sides pursue unjust objectives in continuation of reactionary policy. But no war can exist in which both sides uphold a just policy. Only one side can have just objectives, a policy that conforms to the class or national interests of workers and peasants, of all the working people. These interests are the criteria of the socio-political nature of all wars, both global and local. Lenin said that Communists and all the working people should support just wars and resolutely oppose unjust wars, making every effort to prevent reactionary forces from starting these wars.

While calling upon Marxists and all other progressive forces to support just wars, Lenin militated against interpreting the thesis of a just war in a Leftist, adventurist spirit. Dogmatists,* for instance, assert that inasmuch as war is a continuation of politics, the countries where the working people are in power must fight "revolutionary wars" and that there can be no question of peaceful co-existence of states with different social systems.

Concepts of this kind are provocative and have nothing in common with Marxism. The working people are not indifferent to the price that mankind will have to pay for the right to live in freedom. The forces of progress and their vanguard, the Communist Parties, which are not daunted by any difficulties in the struggle for the interests of the masses, are deeply concerned with the destiny of millions of people. World wars, it will be recalled, have cost mankind tens of millions of lives. Lecturing on *War and Revolution* in May 1917 Lenin stressed that "war is not a game, it is an appalling thing, taking toll of millions of lives . . ." He considered that world wars harboured the danger of undermining "the very foundations of human society."

A world war involving the use of missiles and nuclear weapons, if it is ever started by the imperialists, would destroy all vestiges of the imperialist system but it would, at the same time, inflict colossal damage on the productive forces of modern society: entire countries would be laid waste and the major centres of world production and culture would be reduced to heaps of ruins. This is by no means in the interests of the working class. The working class is interested in preserving the material

requisites for the transition to socialism that have been created by the labour of many generations.

Marxists-Leninists believe that the abolition of imperialist rule and the transition to socialism can be achieved through the development of all forms of the class struggle and the accomplishment of the socialist revolution under conditions of peace between socialist countries and countries with the outworn capitalist system.

While further developing Marxist theory, Lenin said that the working class and its allies could fight imperialism, achieve socialism and democracy and protect their vital class and national interests in various ways, including war. In the article *A Retrograde Trend in Russian Social-Democracy,* written in 1899 and first published in 1924, he wrote: "The working class would, of course, prefer to take power *peacefully* . . . but to *renounce* the revolutionary seizure of power would be *madness* on the part of the proletariat. . . ."

For the working class and all working people the settlement of class or national contradictions through war, through the continuation of politics by violent means, Lenin stressed, is an extreme measure. This measure is resorted to when it is impossible to uphold or defend interests by non-military means, without an armed struggle. In the cases of the progressive forces violence is always a retaliatory, lawful and just reaction to violence by oppressors. Therefore, Lenin said, the attitude to war is a political problem, for politics is, in fact, the destiny of millions of people.

In Lenin's writings there are statements that war could be a factor facilitating the maturing of revolution. During a war social contradictions grow acute and the people mature much more quickly for a struggle ideologically, politically and organisationally. As a result a revolutionary situation thus emerges and it can only end in a proletarian revolution. Lenin therefore had every reason to declare that in Russia the socialist revolution was accelerated by the First World War.

But this does not imply that the Octo-

---

* In this context "dogmatists" refers to the Chinese Communists. In the subsequent five paragraphs the author attacks the militant Chinese interpretation of Lenin's ideas on world revolution, counterposing to it the customary Soviet argument that Lenin regarded coexistence between communism and capitalism as desirable and possible. Both readings of Lenin are correct, Lenin having altered his tactical stance as he thought the international situation required. [Editor's note.]

ber Revolution was the result of that war. Moreover, war is by no means an indispensable condition for accomplishing a socialist revolution. Had it been otherwise, Lenin and the Bolshevik Party would not have opposed the unleashing of the First World War or stigmatised the German, Russian and other Socialist conciliators who voted in favour of granting the bourgeois governments credits for the conduct of the war.

As soon as war broke out, Lenin and the other Bolsheviks called upon the working people of Russia, the soldiers and the sailors to use the military situation in their own class interests by turning their guns against their oppressors, who had started the war.

Like Marx and Engels, Lenin considered that the main motive force of the transition from one social system to another was not war between nations but the class struggle and its culminating point, the social revolution. In 1919 he said that to set the task of overthrowing world imperialism by a violent "export of revolution" would have been "sheer absurdity and nonsense and complete ignorance of the conditions under which the policy of force is successful." He emphasised that "a revolution that follows and is connected with a war . . . is a *particularly severe* case of childbirth."

After the October Revolution he expounded and substantiated the thesis that all governments had to pursue a policy of peaceful coexistence. He regarded world peace as the key to social progress and the building of socialism and communism.

He pointed out that the reasons for war in the 20th century lay solely in the economy and policies of imperialism. But he rejected the idea that wars were inevitable under imperialism and underlined the tremendous role played by the conscious activity and struggle of the masses, who, given certain conditions, could by their resolute action force the imperialist aggressors to renounce world wars as a vehicle of the piratical policy of monopoly capitalism. One of these conditions is, in our day, the presence of the world socialist system headed by the Soviet Union. The socialist camp has placed its economic, moral, political and military power in the service of peace.

Lenin clearly defined the tasks of the revolutionary struggle, the struggle for peace and the armed defence of the socialist motherland.

As long as the threat of imperialist intervention existed, he said, the victorious proletariat had to be in constant combat readiness. For that reason he always gave his attention to problems connected with the conduct of war. War, he said, was governed by its own objective laws, and to ignore these laws meant inviting defeat. Among these laws he singled out the . . . dependence of the course and outcome of a war . . . on the . . . correlation of material and spiritual forces available to the belligerents. Victory in war, he said, goes to the side that has greater reserves, greater sources of strength, greater endurance deep down among the people.

He pinpointed the direct dependence of the course and outcome of a war on . . . the qualitative features of the personnel. In an article entitled "The Fall of Port Arthur" (1905) he noted that "wars today are fought by peoples" and require "high-quality manpower." He further noted that no matter how high the level of endurance and physical strength is, it cannot give superiority in the epoch of rapid-firing small arms, rapid-firing cannon and technical means, and that the masses play the decisive role in war in comparison with technical means. The better the technical means that man has at his disposal and the more skilfully they are utilised, the stronger he becomes.

Lenin attached the greatest importance to the role, formation and sociopolitical nature of the moral-political factor in war. Addressing a conference of workers and Red Army men in Moscow on May 13, 1920, he said: "In the final analysis, victory in any war depends on the spirit animating the masses that spill their own blood on the field of battle. The conviction that the war is in a just cause and the realisation that their lives must be laid down for the welfare of their brothers strengthen the morale of the fighting men and enable them to endure incredible hardships."

Lenin considered the state of the rear as one of the paramount factors contributing towards the victorious outcome of a war. The people most devoted to the revolution, he said, would be immediately annihilated if they were not sufficiently well armed, supplied with food and trained. Besides, no war, he emphasised, was possible without the most serious economic preparations. The strength of the rear, he believed, was determined by the socio-political system and by the nature and objectives of the war. He stressed that in war victory was achieved by tensing all of a nation's economic and organisational strength.

On the eve of the Great October Revolution he wrote an article—"Can the Bolsheviks Retain State Power?"—in which he pointed out that "the defence potential of a country that has thrown off the yoke of capital, that has given the peasants land and has placed the banks and factories under workers' control would be *many times* greater than the defence potential of a capitalist country," and that "the class that can lead the mass of the population must triumph historically." Such a class is the working class which is capable of rallying around it all working people, above all the peasantry, and leading them in the fight for social and national liberation, for the victory of democracy and socialism. Lenin taught that the alliance of the working class and working peasantry was the decisive social and political force capable of repulsing any attack on the part of both external and internal counter-revolutionaries. At the same time, he considered that it was of paramount impor-

tance to assess the enemy correctly, to refrain from letting success turn one's head, and to make every effort to strengthen the defence power of the victorious revolution.

Lenin said that one had to regard the conduct of war as an art. Lenin's propositions on leadership in a war form an important part of his military legacy. The draft directives of the Party Central Committee on military unity, written by Lenin, state that there must be the strictest centralisation in the utilisation of all the forces and resources of socialist republics. During a war all institutions, he said, had to be geared to the requirements of the front and each person had to be made responsible for a precisely defined job. Lenin repeatedly pointed out that the working class had to train its own highly efficient commanding cadres, otherwise it "would fail to master combat equipment and methods of modern warfare."

Lenin's works on military problems contain a profoundly scientific, Marxist analysis of wars in the epoch of imperialism and generalise the experience of the revolutionary struggle of the world and, in particular, the Russian proletariat. Lenin creatively developed the Marxist theory of war and armies, defined the attitude of the proletarian Party to wars and military affairs, showed the class nature and features of wars in the modern epoch, exposed imperialism as the only force responsible for armed conflicts and wars, scientifically proved that civil and national-liberation wars of the working people were just, elucidated the purpose and nature of the armed forces of the proletarian state and demonstrated the historic need for defending the socialist Motherland by force of arms.

II. REVOLUTIONARY TACTICIAN

Max Eastman

ENGINEER OF REVOLUTION

Max Eastman, born in 1883, was a prominent editor in the American Left from 1913 to 1922. He rose to international renown largely as a result of his stay in Soviet Russia from 1922 to 1924 and the strange role he came to play in the Bolshevik succession crisis that followed upon Lenin's death. Trying to help his friend Trotsky against mounting intrigue, he published his book *Since Lenin Died,* in which he leaked the news of Lenin's testament that Trotsky had secretly told him about while he was still inside Russia. After Trotsky's expulsion from the U.S.S.R., Eastman translated most of his major writings into English, including the monumental *History of the Russian Revolution.* Eastman himself wrote several books attacking Stalinism, including *The End of Socialism in Russia* and *Stalin's Russia and the Crisis in Socialism.* In 1941 Eastman became a roving editor for the *Reader's Digest.* He died in 1969.

IF you wanted to build a bridge across a stream, it would be absurd to make your calculations upon the assumption that the properties of steel and iron are such that they are going across the stream, and that you are lending consciousness to the process. It would not require a book to demonstrate that this was a relic of animism. In creating a dictatorship of the proletariat, as a bridge toward a real human society, the absurdity of this way of calculating is less obvious, but it is equally great. The only difference here is that the material you work with is moving, and it is human, and you are a part of it. This does not alter the nature of thought and purposive action, or justify you in regarding yourself as a reflecting apparatus, instead of an engineer. It merely gives rise to a large and altogether peculiar set of engineering problems. And it was exactly these problems which Lenin solved, and whose solution created the "Bolshevik" departure in Marxism. Lenin's fundamental contribution to the Marxian science was a determination of the way in which engineers who use it, must relate

themselves to the moving human material of which they are a part.

Bolshevism, like so many other things, can be best understood by studying it at the point of origin. It was born in Lenin's attack upon a school of compromising Marxists who called themselves "Economists." Their idea was that the Marxian intellectuals in Russia ought not to alienate the workers by stressing the political aspect of the revolution, the necessity of overthrowing the czar's government, but ought simply to enter into the economic struggle with the bosses, leaving these political changes to follow in the natural course of events. They ought to subordinate themselves to the spontaneous, or as they called it "elemental," movement of the workers. Lenin destroyed this humble-casuistical tendency completely in his journal "Iskra" and his book *What to Do?* He put in its place the idea of an "organization of professional revolutionists," who, while welding themselves into a dynamic identity with the elemental movement of the workers, should nevertheless retain their own organizational identity, and their own intellectual

From Max Eastman, *Marx, Lenin, and the Science of Revolution* (London: George Allen and Unwin Ltd., 1926), pp. 141–154, 157–160, 167–168. Reprinted by permission of the publisher.

identity—their unqualified and undissembled loyalty to the whole programme of political and economic revolution. He maintained that such an organization was not only advisable, but indispensable to victory. "I assert," he said, "that no revolutionary movement can be durable without a solid organization of leaders capable of maintaining their succession."

In his further development and the development of his party, Lenin ceased to employ the concept of "professional revolutionist." It was a peculiarly Russian concept—the essential fruit, indeed, of that consecrated movement of revolt which had preceded Bolshevism in Russia. And Lenin apparently knew that it was Russian. He knew that it was out of accord with the Marxian manner of thinking as it had developed in western Europe. He always resisted the proposal to translate into other languages the book in which he had laid down the foundations of Bolshevism. But he never yielded to those in Russia who accused him of having exaggerated in that book the rôle of these "professional revolutionists." He replied that their rôle *had been* indispensable, and he explained the disappearance of this concept from his writings of a later date, by saying that the "professional revolutionist has done his work in the history of Russian proletarian socialism." He has succeeded, that is, in welding himself into a dynamic unity with the elemental struggle of the workers, so that the organization ultimately formed can be treated as a single unit, the "vanguard" of the revolutionary proletariat. By an adroit use of this word "vanguard," Lenin reconciled his language in later years with that of western European Marxism. But I believe no Bolshevik would deny that the professional revolutionist continued, during the growth and triumph of Lenin's party, to play the same indispensable rôle that was ascribed to him at its foundation. In the official "History of the Russian Communist Party," published during Lenin's life, we read:

If you inquire, from the standpoint of the personal staff of leaders, what our party lives by at the present time, and even our

state, it will become clear that to a significant degree even now after twenty years, the party so to speak, nourishes itself upon that group of professional revolutionists, the foundations of which were laid at the beginning of the century.

The concept of professional revolutionist belongs, then, not only to the origin, but to the essence of Bolshevism. And if you will reflect how directly a person's "class" depends upon his "profession," you will see that to make revolution itself a "profession," was a very real departure in a philosophy which regards revolution as an automatic outcome of the struggle of classes. To declare that the people of that "profession" are indispensable to the victory of the working class, has the appearance of heresy. And this appearance becomes more pronounced when you learn that, in describing his professional revolutionists, Lenin repeatedly declared that "it makes no difference" whether they belong to the working class or not.

The organization of revolutionists ought to embrace first of all and chiefly people whose profession consists of revolutionary activity. . . . And before this general title of member of the organization, all distinction between workers and intelligentsia should be obliterated, to say nothing of distinctions between this and that separate profession.

Thus Lenin founded his Bolshevik organization upon a recognition of the *indispensable* historic function of a group of people who were not defined according to the economic class to which they belonged, but were defined according to their purposive activity and their state of mind. They were people committed and consecrated to a certain social purpose —but with this difference, from the "Narodniki," that they possessed the Marxian science and the Marxian technique for the achievement of that purpose. In short, they were scientific revolutionary engineers.

Lenin was accused by other Marxists of "Jacobinism" and "Blanquism" on the ground of this heresy, and I think the accusation should have been accepted.

Lenin was amazingly contented, or rather determined, to attribute all of his wisdom to Karl Marx. It seemed to fulfill some need of his emotional nature to do so. But a mature history of his policies would neglect neither his own contributions nor those of the great French revolutionists. Lenin corrected the error of Marx, which was a mystic faith in the proletariat as such; and he corrected the error of Blanqui, which was to trust all to the organization of revolutionists. He saw that the organization of revolutionists must be actually rooted in, and welded together with, the proletariat by a whole series of personal and organizational bonds, so that they not only assume to represent the proletariat, but also, when a revolutionary period arrives, actually do represent it. But he saw also that they must be a distinct body of men who "stand above society," and are thus able to understand it. And his arrant insistence upon centralized authority and military discipline in that body of men, smacks more of the tactics of Blanqui than of the philosophy of Marx.

Moreover, in discussing the part to be played by this organization of revolutionists, Lenin contradicted the Marxian metaphysics and abandoned it absolutely. He abandoned all the confused ideological dodges of the priest of economic metaphysics, who is "bringing to the working class a consciousness of its destiny," and adopted the attitude of a practical artisan who is doing work, and doing it scientifically, and not seriously deceiving himself either about the historic destiny of his material, or the essentially decorative function of his own brain and volition.

* * *

Lenin had no sooner formed his party round a nucleus of "professional revolutionists"—defined and selected according to the purposive ideas in their minds —than he proceeded to split it upon the question whether people of a certain type should be allowed to consider themselves members. And these people again were not defined according to their economic class. They were defined according to their attitude to these purposive ideas. They were the people who talk revolution, and like to think about it, but do not "mean business." They were the "soft" as opposed to the "hard," the "reasoners" as opposed to the "fighters," the "talkers" as opposed to the "workers." Lenin proposed to eliminate them by demanding that every party member should work under the orders of the conspirative organization, accepting the full risk and discipline involved. Martov proposed a "more elastic" definition of a party member. Upon this issue the party split into "Bolsheviks" and "Mensheviks." Martov and his followers turned out to be themselves people of just the type Lenin wanted to exclude—people who talked revolution but did not intend to produce it. And therefore the very meaning of these words "Bolshevik" and "Menshevik," is to be found in that sharp psychological distinction made by Lenin at the beginning of his career.

Better that ten workers should not call themselves members of the party (real workers are not so eager for position) than that one talker should have the right and the opportunity to be a party member. There is the principle which seems to me irrefutable, and which compels me to fight against Martov.

Lenin subsequently fought these Mensheviks upon a great variety of questions, and he attempted to define them in ways more in accord with the economic metaphysics. But the one element in their position which never changed, and which alone makes it possible to define them, is this psychological one. They were always seeking a formula which would enable them to talk revolution without incurring the danger of realizing it.

Thus Lenin's first innovation was to recognize the indispensable function of the man of ideas, his second innovation was to divide men of ideas into two camps, and expel without mercy those in whom ideas do not mean action. It is plain, then, that Lenin did not regard revolutionary ideas as a mere reflection of the evolution of the forces of production. A talker is just as good a reflecting apparatus as a worker. Indeed, the very use of the word "work" in order to make this all-important distinction, is a denial of the philosophy according to which revolution is an automatic product of nature's development. For work, according to the definition of Marx himself, is "a process between man and nature, in which man through his own act adjusts, regulates and controls his material intercourse with nature. He opposes himself to nature as one of her own forces. . . ." A Bolshevik, then, according to the distinction originally made by Lenin himself, is a man of Marxian ideas who opposes himself to nature with a view to regulation and control. And is there any better definition of a Menshevik than a man of Marxian ideas who is willing to let nature regulate and control him, so long as he is allowed to express and cherish these ideas?

In forming his revolutionary party, Lenin identified and excluded another type of revolutionist whose attitude he described as the "Infantile Disease of Leftism." This distinction was also fundamentally a psychological one, as the name implies. But, unlike the distinction between Menshevik and Bolshevik, it was originally formulated by Lenin in terms of economic class, and only received this more concrete definition in later years. At the time when Lenin formed his party, practically all the "Infantile Leftists" in Russia were opposed to Marxism itself. They found their natural place in the terrorist wing of the Narodniki, and the Narodniki denied, along with the entire Marxian system, the importance of the industrial proletariat. They believed in "the people"; and the people, numerically speaking, were quite obviously the small peasant proprietors. For this reason it was possible at that time to identify and define the "infantile leftist" in orthodox Marxian fashion as a "petit bourgeois revolutionist." Later on, when this same psychological phenomenon appeared in Lenin's own proletarian party, the economic designation gave place more and more to the psychological. The name "revolutionists of the phrase" became a very important one with Lenin. And in 1908 a whole group was expelled from his party for the

merely tactical crime of refusing to sit in a bourgeois parliament. They were described at that time as "Leftists." And in 1920, when as a result of the successful revolution in Russia this same phenomenon made its appearance throughout the whole Bolshevik International, and became a serious menace to the tactics of the proletarian struggle, Lenin wrote his famous pamphlet defining it as "The Infantile Disease of Leftism," and denouncing it almost exclusively in psychological terms. . . .

He shows these Leftists that, while they may be emotionally sincere, they are intellectually immature. They do not know how to think practically. He describes them at various points as "abstract," "sectarian," as substituting "purity of principle" for practicality of tactics, as following a "tactic of mere negation," of "opposition on principle," satisfying themselves with "mere words," with "revolutionary moods and dispositions." He demonstrates the impracticality of their characteristic policies, *no compromise, down with leaders, abstention from bourgeois parliaments and reactionary trade unions, individual terrorism, illegality-for-its-own-sake,* and the like. In short he explains to them, not as a representative of the proletariat talking to representatives of the petite bourgeoisie, but as a teacher talking to his pupils, what practical thinking is, and how to do it. The real definition of "Infantile Leftism," as it is implied throughout the body of Lenin's pamphlet, seems to me to be this: It is an attitude of immature revolutionary minds, who judge ideas and policies as an expression of the revolutionary motive and emotion, rather than as a means of achieving the revolution.

*   *   *

Lenin is alleged to have profoundly modified Marxism as a theory by recognizing the peasants and the oppressed colonial peoples as "allies" of the working class in its struggle. And yet this assertion always has to be accompanied by the remark that Marx also recognized the peasants and the colonial peoples as allies of the working class in its struggle. What then is the modification introduced by Lenin? Simply this, that being profoundly indifferent to the metaphysical picture of the revolution as automatically produced by a resolution of "contradictions" involved in the development of industrial capitalism, Lenin was able to see the industrial proletariat, the peasants, and the colonial peoples, in their true *practical* proportions. Marx saw them in the proportions determined by a dialectic construction of which the peasants and the colonial peoples are not a perfectly integral part. Therefore his recognition of them as "allies" was incidental and inadequate in comparison with Lenin's. Marx was a metaphysician accommodating his metaphysics in a parenthesis to the demands of practical science; Lenin was a practical scientist, ignoring altogether the metaphysics in which he believed. That is the essential difference between Lenin and Marx, so far as concerns the peasants and the colonial peoples.

The most striking feature of Lenin's political tactics was the "policy of sharp turns." Lenin would adopt a programme, or a slogan, sufficiently fundamental to serve among ordinary politicians as the corner-stone of a republic, or the motto of a "Grand Old Party" through several generations, and then he would appear some morning a short while later and say: "The situation has changed, our programme has no further value, the slogan for the present period is as follows. . . ." Nothing like this had ever been seen before. It makes most of the great liberators appear a little wooden, a little out of gear with reality, in comparison with Lenin. It contributed more than anything else to make his political power seem occult and almost magical. And yet it was the opposite of magic; it was the essence of scientific engineering introduced into the sphere of politics. I have shown that the distinction between scientific engineering and the practice of magic, whether in the matter of producing gold or in the matter of producing a true society, lies in the scientists' recognition and definition of an unchangeable or uncontrollable element in the given

facts. There is, however, this great difference between an engineer of human history, applying the principles of Marxism, and a chemical or physical engineer— the engineer of history works with a material which is itself spontaneously changing, and he with it, in ways not irrelevant to his purpose. He cannot define once for all, except in the most general terms, the factual conditions limiting and prescribing his action. He cannot keep these conditions constant. He must therefore continually revert to the conditions, and continually redefine them, amending his procedure according to the new elements which are beyond his control. That is the significance of the "policy of sharp turns." It is a proof that Lenin was in the full sense of the term a scientific engineer. The conjurer survived in him no more than the priest.

Lenin's Marxian eulogists usually point to the soviet form of government as the essential expression of his creative genius. The superficiality of this judgment becomes apparent when you know that during the months preceding the October revolution, pursuing his essential policy of sharp turns, Lenin was once on the point of abandoning altogether the slogan "All Power to the soviets!" The essential expression of Lenin's genius was the creation of an organization of purposive revolutionists capable of standing above and outside all such specific forms and formulations, using them or discarding them according to their transitory relation to a more general social purpose. Lenin left to "history" the decision whether the revolution should flow in the channel of the soviets or not. But he did not leave to history the decision whether the revolution should be led by the Bolshevik party. He did not leave to history the creation of that party, nor the maintenance of its entirely extraordinary character and policy. If he had, there would have been no Bolshevik revolution, as Trotsky in his "Lessons of October" has very effectively shown. I believe that no organization of men ever before exercised so profound an influence upon history in exactly the direction planned by it as the Russian Communist Party. It is an organization of a kind which never existed before. It combines certain essential features of a political party, a professional association, a consecrated order, an army, a scientific society—and yet is in no sense a sect. Instead of cherishing in its membership a sectarian psychology, it cherishes a certain relation to the predominant class-forces of society as Marx defined them. And this relation was determined by Lenin, and progressively readjusted by him, with a subtlety of which Marx never dreamed.

* * *

To me the fundamental difference between Marx and Lenin is visible on almost every page they wrote. It is not a contradiction, but a difference of mental attitude. And it is not a complete difference, because Marx had in him the practical scientist, and Lenin never consciously got rid of the metaphysician. But it is a difference of all the more importance to Marxians. It may be summed up in the following two quotations about the dictatorship of the proletariat:

Marx says: "The new thing that I did consisted in demonstrating . . . that the class struggle inevitably leads to the dictatorship of the proletariat."

Lenin says: "Marx's teaching about the class struggle leads inevitably to a recognition . . . [that] the overthrow of the bourgeoisie is attainable only through the transformation of the proletariat into a ruling class."

Marx states that such a thing will happen in such a way. Lenin states that such is the only way to make it happen. Marx attributes his purpose to the external world, and tries to convert the facts and methods of action which make its realization possible, into a proof of its certainty. Lenin assumes that the revolutionary purpose exists in revolutionary people, and shows them those facts in the external world, and those methods of action, which make its realization possible. In Marx the Hegelian metaphysician was dominant over the practical scientific thinker; in Lenin the scientific thinker gained the victory. And that victory is the theoretical foundation of Bolshevism. Bolshevism is an unconscious, and therefore incomplete, substitution of a practical science of revolution for that revolutionary philosophy of the universe which Marx created.

Stanley W. Page

PROPHET OF EASTERN REVOLUTION

Stanley W. Page is Professor of History at the City College and the City University of New York. His scholarly interest has focused mainly on Lenin and on the past century of Russian and Soviet history. His books include *Lenin and World Revolution, Russia In Revolution,* and *The Formation of the Baltic States.* This reading, drawn mainly from one of Professor Page's articles, demonstrates Lenin's political realism, his ability, when necessity demanded, to part company even with one of Marxism's most basic tenets; namely, that the socialist world revolution would have to begin in the industrialized West.

ONE of the earliest prophets of Asia in revolt was Lenin. Throughout most of his life he confidently expected a world revolution born in the West, as originally predicted by Marx. But the logic of overpowering circumstance forced Lenin, just prior to his death, to admit that the world revolution would emerge from the East.

In 1902 Lenin wrote that Russia would be the initial point of world upheaval. The proletarian-led overthrow of the Tsar, he claimed, would set in revolutionary motion not only the working classes of the Western nations but also the peoples of Asia. What impelled the hard-headed Lenin to cast the Russian proletariat in so grandiose an international rôle? Essentially it was the realization that even if the proletariat of Russia led a successful revolution against the autocracy and then seized power, it could not bring socialism to agrarian Russia. If the proletarian party could not possibly produce a socialist society, then what claim did it, or its self-appointed leader, Lenin, have to inclusion in the ranks of the Marxists? Lenin discovered the Russian proletarian party's Marxist reason for existence in the Western revolution, for which Russia would be the beacon. The victorious Western proletariat would then turn to Russia and help build up her industry and technology, thus paving the way for socialism in Russia. In 1902 Lenin, to all appearances, included the Asiatic revolution in his thinking for good measure. At the time he considered it the less important part of his famous prophecy, but it turned out to be of greater consequence than his speculations on the Western revolution.

Despite the failure of the parties of the working class to achieve their goals in the Russian Revolution of 1905, Lenin claimed or implied on numerous later occasions that 1905 had inspired a chain reaction of revolutionary incidents affecting almost every corner of Asia. In October of 1908, commenting on the Young Turk revolt and the concomitant risings in Azerbaidjan, Lenin wrote that the "awakening to political life of the Asiatic peoples received special impetus from the Russo-Japanese War and the Russian Revolution [of 1905]." In his comment of subsequent years on Asiatic revolt, Lenin omitted all reference to the Japanese victory (probably because this would have weakened his argument regarding the effect of the Russian Revolution) and, simultaneously, stressed his estimate of the impact of 1905 upon Asia.

From Stanley W. Page, "Lenin: Prophet of World Revolution from the East," *The Russian Review,* April 1952, pp. 67–75 and from *Lenin and World Revolution* (New York, New York University Press, 1959), pp. 143–146. Reprinted by permission of the publishers.

A very good case could be drawn up to prove that the original irritants of the Russian Revolution and the Asiatic revolutionary movements were such Western stimuli as nationalism and the industrial revolution. Nevertheless, during the years following 1905, Lenin, unlike other Marxists, took an almost proprietary interest in anything resembling popular insurgence in Asia, allowing few incidents to pass without exhaustive comment. Usually Lenin spoke encouragingly of these movements and attempted to link them in some way with the concept of world revolution.

Why should Lenin, Marxist that he was, have taken such note of democratic stirrings in Asia? Essentially this was part and parcel of his campaign to demonstrate that even if the proletarian-led Revolution of 1905 had not overthrown the Tsar, it had still succeeded, for it established the correct pattern for the next revolution. Among other things, it had, in the Moscow insurrection of December, provided the first modern example of militant working-class martyrdom since the Paris Commune. Besides this, said Lenin in effect as he pointed to Asia, the Revolution of 1905 had given the predicted impulsion to world revolution. It was all the more necessary for Lenin to stress the Asiatic revolutions, since the Western proletariat, which Lenin had relied upon to bring socialism to Russia, had remained all too unresponsive to the events of 1905 in Russia.

At the same time, due credit must be given Lenin as the sole Marxist of his day to regard the Asiatic masses as desirous of rights very similar to those demanded by underprivileged members of Western society, and to recognize their potentialities for popular revolution. This fact demands closer attention. Marxist though he was, Lenin was also a Russian. The Russians, whose country straddles Europe and Asia, have always understood the Asiatic mind better than have the Westerners. In addition to this, Lenin was a Marxist in a land of peasants. Since he desired violent overthrow of the Russian government, he had to concede the importance, however secondary in terms of leadership, of the revolutionary force

of an aroused peasantry. It was Lenin who in 1905 first advanced the thesis, so alien to orthodox Marxism and to Trotsky, that the Russian revolution could be won only by a peasant-proletariat alliance. The inference here is that Lenin, unable to conceive of a revolution in Russia without participation of the peasants, by the same token, sensed the revolutionary potential of the Asiatic countries. Although these lands possessed virtually no industrial proletariat, they were actually not far behind Russia, whose industrial revolution, even by 1917, was still in its infancy.

It was the Chinese movement which interested Lenin the most—and for good reasons. The Chinese Revolution, as Lenin saw it, was, in many of its facets, the Russian Revolution of 1905 transplanted to the land of the Manchus. China's upheaval was, in fact, not led by the proletariat; China had no industry. But the Revolution of 1911 succeeded, where the Russian masses had failed, in overthrowing the monarchy through a collaboration of bourgeois liberals and peasants. As Lenin pointed out in 1912, "Chinese freedom was won by a union of peasant democracy and bourgeois liberalism. Whether the peasants, not led by a proletarian party, would be able to support their democratic position against the liberals, who await only the appropriate moment to turn to the right, remains to be seen."

In the Chinese movement, Lenin reserved special esteem for the Nationalist Kuomintang Party, headed by Sun-Yat-Sen. This party Lenin regarded as analogous to the *Narodniki*, revolutionaries of the corresponding historical period in Russia, who dreamed that their motherland might skip the capitalist way-station on her road to socialism. It seems evident from this that Lenin was further interested in Asia because in those retrograde areas of the world he perceived laboratory conditions directly applicable to the Russian agrarian scene and hence worth studying. From the political standpoint, the parallels drawn by Lenin between Russian and Asiatic revolution might instill optimism among the Bolshevik following, downcast as it was by the lack of revolutionary reverberations of 1905 in Europe.

The marked social and political ferment in pre-1914 Asia contrasted so sharply with pre-war Europe that Lenin, disquieted perhaps, found himself constrained, in May, 1913, to write an article in *Pravda* entitled "Backward Europe and Progressive Asia."

In Asia, everywhere, he wrote,

the mighty democratic movement grows, spreads, and strengthens itself. [In Asia] the bourgeoisie still moves with the people against the feudal reaction. [National independence or unity not having been achieved by Asiatic countries, the bourgeoisie, from the Marxist viewpoint, still played a constructive role.] Hundreds of millions of people are there awakening to life, to light, to freedom. What joy this world movement evokes in the hearts of all conscientious workers, knowing that the path to collectivism lies through democracy —with what feelings of sympathy for young Asia are all honest democrats filled. But . . . progressive Europe [this reference to the European bourgeoisie was meant sarcastically] robs China and helps the enemies of democracy, the enemies of freedom in China. All those who rule Europe, the entire bourgeoisie, are united with all the forces of reaction and feudalism [medievalism] in China. However, all of young Asia, *i.e.*, the hundreds of millions of toilers of Asia, have a trustworthy ally in the person of the proletariat of all the civilized countries. No power on earth can prevent their victory, which will liberate not only the peoples of Europe [and Russia] but also the peoples of Asia.

Whatever the dormant nature of the Western proletariat, and in 1905 Lenin attributed it to exhaustion from the long struggle against bourgeois reaction, the power and the will to revolt was inherent in it. The West, as Marx had proven, was going to do the really heavy work of the world revolution and would save the Asiatics from the Western bourgeoisie and their reactionary allies. The spark of 1905 had seemingly failed to detonate the powder magazine. A bigger spark was nascent as 1914 approached.

When World War I broke out, Lenin believed that capitalism's hour of doom had struck. He expected that the socialist parties of each country would seize the opportunity afforded by the arming of the working class and instruct their faithful flocks to turn their weapons against their own governments instead of those of their supposed enemies. Civil strife everywhere instead of international imperialist war would be the result. This would bring about the world revolution and the unity of the proletariat called for by the Communist Manifesto. But Lenin was doomed to disappointment. The socialists of the various countries chose to rally to their national banners rather than fight against them.

In 1916, Lenin, pacing restlessly in Swiss exile and impatiently awaiting the revolution which should have been breaking in war-torn Western Europe, wrote his well-known work, *Imperialism, the Highest Stage of Capitalism*. This pamphlet, composed between January and July of 1916, coincident with the dialectical squabbles surrounding the Kienthal Conference held on April 24, was intended to prove beyond question that imperialist wars were inevitable outgrowths of capitalism. Therefore, to end such wars, no compromise with capitalism was permissible on the part of the working-class leaders. That is to say, the left socialist movement must contemplate no peace based upon the continuing existence of bourgeois governments. This would be foolish in any case, since, as Lenin's work explained, imperialism as the dying phase of capitalism was also the prelude to world revolution.

"The tens of millions of dead and maimed left by the 'war,'" wrote Lenin in the preface to the French edition of his book, ". . . open the eyes of the tens of millions of people who are downtrodden, oppressed . . . and duped by the bourgeoisie, with unprecedented rapidity. Thus out of the universal ruin caused by a war, a worldwide revolutionary crisis is arising which . . . cannot end in any other way than in a proletarian revolution and its victory."

Having proved the revolution imminent, Lenin had to explain what still supported the rotten house of capitalism. This survived, he postulated, because of the "enormous super-profits" gained by plundering the whole world. These made it possible for the imperialists "to *bribe* the labor leaders and the upper stratum of the labor aristocracy. . . . This stratum of workers, becoming bourgeoisie . . . who are quite philistine in their mode of life, in the size of their earnings and in their outlook, serves as the principal prop of the Second International, and, in our days, the principal social (not military) *prop of the bourgeoisie*." According to Lenin, then, world revolution was just below the horizon, though temporarily delayed by the treacherous leaders of the Second International. However, Lenin hopefully pointed to the diminished possibility that labor would attain its ends through "opportunistic" methods. In England, for instance, competition from other countries had, in the last decades, greatly lessened the superprofits of English capitalism.

Lenin held out one prospect for the future. Even if no important revolutionary events were forthcoming from the European war, there was that long-range Achilles heel of capitalism, the effects of imperialism upon the subject peoples of the world's colonies. Lenin, here citing R. Hilferding's *Das Finanzkapital* verbatim, shows how imperialism was creating conditions dangerous to itself in a colonial world awakening to national consciousness. In addition to providing the colonial peoples with a rallying point for their xenophobia, imperialism also gave them means and resources (industry, training in modern warfare) for the achievement of the national state as a means to economic and cultural freedom. Having secured these ends, they could take up the anti-imperialist struggle. This last point Lenin hardly intended as anything for Bolsheviks to rely upon. It emerges in his treatise as a bare whisper, perhaps as a final justification of the correctness of Marxist thought, even if all else should fail for the time being. Whatever its soundness, Lenin could not have wished to stress it. The correct Marxist-Bolshevik view, as he saw it, was the expectation of more or less imminent revolution in the West.

All thought of Asia was pretty well shelved after the abdication of Nicholas II in March, 1917. Here indeed was the moment Lenin had dreamed of in 1902. Lenin returned to Russia on April 16 to take over active leadership of the Bolsheviks. He advanced the claim that the proletariat, in line with his prophecies of 1902–1905, had assumed the guiding rôle in the overthrow of the autocracy. This point was, at best, highly contestable. But if Lenin, in the face of overwhelming evidence to the contrary, could convince himself of the fact that his early prognostication had been brilliantly fulfilled, then it was surely no task for him to foresee the materialization of the next step in the prophecy— proletarian revolution in the West, sparked by proletarian-led overthrow of the monarchy in Russia.

In 1905, Lenin had disagreed with Trotsky over the manner in which a revolutionary government, once it had seized power, ought to behave with respect to world revolution. Lenin held that the overthrow of the monarchy and the bourgeoisie, by virtue of the proletarian-led peasant-proletarian alliance, was all that could be expected of the Russian Revolution. The task of the revolutionary republic, as Lenin saw it, would then be to hold power until the European revolution, incited by that of Russia, took form. The European cataclysm thus unleashed would then rescue the Russian Revolution, while bringing into Russia the technology needed to make Russia socialist. Trotsky had contended that the numerically predominant peasantry, ridden as it was with bourgeois leanings, could not be relied upon as an ally of the proletariat. The revolutionary forces, once the reins of power were theirs, must actively join the proletariat of Europe in bringing on the revolution. Only an immediately following European revolution, Trotsky believed, could save Russia from counterrevolution aided by outside intervention.

In the summer of 1917, in view of the European war which, after the March revolution, was expected to evoke imminent revolutionary developments, Lenin considered Trotsky's scheme more timely than his own. Consequently, he formed an ideological compact with Trotsky. Once the Bolsheviks had seized power, he virtually abandoned his earlier idea of the proletarian-peasant republic in favor of a dictatorship of the proletariat (his concept of it, at any rate) and proceeded soon after the defeat of Germany to plunge himself and his exhausted forces into the task of bringing Bolshevik order out of the chaos then existing in Central Europe. The Third, or Communist International, called to life by the Bolsheviks in March, 1919, was the organizational instrument for achieving this end. At about that time Bolshevik hopes glowed brightly as Communists seized power in Hungary and Bavaria. Harried as they were by civil war and intervention, the Bolsheviks actually hoped to send military aid to Soviet Hungary.

However, as in 1914, if not in 1905, the Western proletariat again failed Lenin. By the end of 1919, it was becoming increasingly clear that the revolutionary tide was fast receding in Western Europe. But Marxism could not be wrong, and since all the economic preconditions for revolution were at hand, Lenin could permit himself to find but one explanation for its nonoccurrence. The masses, as in 1914–1916, had again been deluded. The labor aristocracy, although forced to make certain verbal concessions to the revolutionary spirit, had by dint of its flexibility managed to maintain control over the proletariat and restrain it from overthrowing the bourgeois fortresses. Now appearing in the guise of centrism, this "aristocracy" was, as ever, linked to the bourgeoisie by bribes derived from imperialist profits. As on earlier occasions, Lenin tried to glean what solace he could from the idea of the "revolutionary East."

Sometime during the period of late summer and fall of 1919 Lenin arrived at a concept regarding the course of world revolution differing radically from that which he had hitherto held. Though continuing to regard the West as the eventual heartland of socialism, he became convinced that revolution in the West would have to be preceded by revolution in Asia. Undoubtedly contributing to his new outlook was the fact that Russian contact with Communist-controlled Turkestan, broken off early in 1918, was re-established in September, 1919, as a result of the collapse of Kolchak's forces. Having at this timely juncture recaptured the gateway to the East, Lenin at once set in feverish motion a campaign to undo the damages done the Soviet eastward face by the Russian Communists who had run the Turkmen Soviets during their period of isolation from Moscow. These Communists had fallen into the ways of the old tsarist bureaucracy. Together with the local magnates they had looted and terrorized the poor, turning them into implacable enemies of the revolution. This situation was duly noted by a commission of Russian Bolsheviks arriving in Tashkent in November.

A decree drawn up by Lenin in October and defining the task of that commission had specified that self-determination of the peoples of Turkestan, "and the abolition of all national inequality and privilege of one national group at the cost of another" was the basis of the entire policy of the Soviet government of Russia. Only such a policy, Lenin had written, could "finally overcome the mistrust of the native working masses of Turkestan, created by the many-yeared domination of Russian tsarism, to the workers and peasants of Russia."

Quite contrary to the spirit expressed in the decree was the letter Lenin wrote to the Turkmen Communists in which he directed them to co-operate with the commission. He explained that the establishment of "correct relations" with the peoples of Turkestan had an immediate significance for the Soviet Republic, which "without exaggeration" could "be described as gigantic and world historical. For all of Asia and for all of the colonies of the world, for a thousand million people, the relations of the Soviet worker-peasant republic to the weak, hitherto oppressed peoples, will have a practical significance." Lenin "very much" begged the Turkmen Communists to "show by deeds the sincerity of our desire to root out all traces of Great Russian imperialism for the supreme struggle with world imperialism headed by that of Britain." The cleanup of Turkestan was aimed primarily to serve as a display advertising Bolshevik egalitarianism throughout the colonial world.

Highly significant at this time was the appearance of a series of articles by Stalin's protégé Mirza Sultan-Galiyev (a Volga-Tatar Communist) in *Zhizn' Natsional 'nostei*, official organ of the Commissariat of Nationalities. These articles, which could scarcely have appeared without Lenin's explicit approval if not encouragement, maintained that Communist leaders had "committed a great strategic blunder by placing the main emphasis in their revolutionary activity in Western Europe. The weakest link in the capitalist chain was not the West but the East, and the failure of communist revolutions abroad was directly attributable to the inadequacy of Soviet efforts in the Eastern borderlands."

On November 22, 1919, Lenin addressed the eighty-two delegates attending the opening session of the Second All-Russian Congress of Communist Organizations of the Peoples of the East. The time had come, he declared, for all the awakening peoples of the East to take part in "deciding the fate of the entire world" and no longer to be "mere objects of [imperialist] enrichment." To develop rapidly, he said, the revolutionary movement of the East would have to tie itself directly to "the revolutionary struggle of our Soviet Republic," whose backwardness, immense extent, and position of link between Europe and Asia gave it the "entire burden" and "great honor" of serving as "the leader of the world struggle against imperialism."

The events of the Russian revolution, Lenin pointed out, could well provide inspiration for the Asiatics. The Red Army's victory proved that a revolutionary war waged by oppressed peoples could be won against "all the wonders of [European] technology and military art." Just as Russia had united its proletariat and peasantry in the struggle against capitalism and the survivals of feudalism, so could an even more backward Asia bring its peasant masses into the struggle "not against capital but against the survivals of feudalism." The unique task facing the Communists of Asia, said Lenin, was that which had faced the Russians, of applying to peculiar conditions, "nonexistent in European countries," the universal Communist theory and practice.

Lenin's speech concluded on the note that only the proletarians of the West could achieve the transition to communism, but that they could not achieve this without the help of the vanguard of Russians plus Asians.

The task is to awaken the toiling masses to revolutionary activity, to conscious action and organization, independent of what level they stand upon; to carry the genuine Communist teaching, intended for the Communists of the more advanced lands, over to the languages of each of the peoples, to achieve the practical tasks which need be achieved quickly and to join in the universal struggle with the proletariat of other countries.

Here are the tasks, whose solutions you will not find in a single Communist pamphlet, but whose solution you will find in the universal struggle which began in Russia. . . . You must base yourselves upon that bourgeois nationalism which is awakening in these peoples. . . . Along with this you must tell [the masses] in language they can understand that the sole hope for freedom lies in the victory of the international revolution and that the international proletariat is the only ally of all the workers and of the exploited hundreds of millions of the peoples of the East.

In June, 1920, a Japanese journalist named Fusse . interviewed Lenin. "Where," he asked Lenin, "does Communism have the best chances for success —in the West or in the East?" Lenin replied, "Genuine Communism can thus far succeed only in the West. However, the West lives on account of the East. European imperialist powers support themselves mainly from Eastern colonies. But at the same time they are arming their colonials and teaching them to fight. Thereby the West is digging its grave in the East."

Essentially, this reply of Lenin's is a restatement of the above-indicated unstressed portion of his *Imperialism*. But it clearly reveals his ambivalent state of mind regarding the potentialities of West and East. The Marxist hope, the foundation for Communism was in the West—but could the workers of Western industry really be counted on? Perhaps, after all, one must wait for the long slow process of Asiatic revolution to run its course and allow capitalism there to dig its own grave.

On September 1, 1920, Lenin bowed further in the general direction of Mecca. By invitation from Moscow, hundreds of delegates convened on that date in Baku. Most came from Moslem countries of Asia and the remarks of Zinoviev, titular leader of the Comintern, were fitted to his audience. In a fiery speech Zinoviev called upon his "brothers" to join the Comintern in a Holy War, "first of all against British imperialism." The Asiatics waved swords, drew daggers, and generally exhibited their enthusiasm for such a project. But, except for causing a ripple of annoyance among British statesmen, this colorful display, at the time, seemed to Western opinion little more than a defiant gesture. To Lenin it was obviously more than that, and within the next three years he was definitely to steer his course in an easterly direction. By 1923 it was fully apparent to him that capitalism had not only not succumbed but was powerful enough and (as Lenin believed) was plotting to strike a fatal blow against the harassed Socialist fatherland. If this were to occur, what would save the world revolution? In one of the last articles he ever put on paper, Lenin held out no hope of rescue by the Western proletariat. Instead, he decisively linked the fate of Soviet Russia and of world revolution to Asia. In the final analysis, Lenin wrote,

The outcome of the struggle depends on the fact that Russia, India, China, etc., contain the vast majority of the world's people. This majority has driven itself ever faster in the last years into the war for its freedom, and, in this sense, there can be no shadow of a doubt as to the eventual decision in the world struggle. In this sense the final victory of socialism is fully and unconditionally guaranteed. . . . In order to secure [Soviet Russia's] existence until

the final military conflict between the counter-revolutionary imperialist West and the revolutionary and nationalist East, between the civilized states of the world and the Eastern remainder, which, however, comprises the majority—it is necessary to succeed in civilizing this majority.

What a contrast this is with 1905, when the Russian Revolution was to be saved by the proletarian revolution in the West! How distant it seems even from 1919, when the Western revolution was already in progress! Indeed, here was a complete break with traditional Marxism, this looking for world revolution from the majority of the world's people instead of from the proletariat of the industrial nations. Such a prognosis of world revolution, however correct it may yet turn out to be, is more worthy of a Malthus than a Marx.

One Bolshevik explanation of this and other Leninist deviations from the Marxist norm has been to describe Leninism as "Marxism in the imperialist era." While there is a good deal of truth in such a description, it is partially an apologetic for having given up the crystallized Marxism which was the basis for much of Bolshevism, while claiming to retain the pristine, orthodox view. It is noteworthy that even Marx, in his last years, had pretty well conceded that proletarian revolutions, even in such advanced countries as England and the United States, were not necessarily inevitable. If Lenin chose to ignore these opinions of Marx for so long it can only be explained in terms of his earlier effort to justify the Russian Marxist party in terms of a Western proletariat waiting for a signal to rise. Lenin was, in this as in every other respect, the Machiavellian politician, ready to seize upon such ideas or slogans as were handy to advance his cause. But Lenin also had a gift immeasurably valuable to the crusader—that of being able to build a personal dogma out of his own rationalizations. Lenin had so long conjured with the thought of Russian revolution as the beginning of Western revolution that he forgot that this had become a truth only through his own faith in it.

With all this, Lenin was too realistic

to cling indefinitely even to self-conceived misconceptions. Thus, when it was clear that the Russian Revolution had not set off revolution in the West and that, consequently, the Western proletariat would not save the Russian Revolution, he was enough of a strategist to retreat and seek reinforcements elsewhere. Reluctantly he abandoned an article of faith that had served him well, and turned his hopes upon the restless stirrings of Asia, where, industry or no industry, world revolution was actually in the making.

Alfreds Berzins

MANIPULATOR OF CAPITALIST NATIONS

Alfreds Berzins was born in Latvia and participated in the Latvian war of liberation that was waged in large part against a communist regime that held power in Latvia for six months in 1919. Berzins was elected a deputy to the Latvian Parliament in 1931 and became Undersecretary of the Interior in 1934 and Minister for Public and Social Affairs in 1936. He was actively involved in the events connected with the Soviet annexation of Latvia in June, 1940. He has described the communist takeover of the Baltic States in his book *The Unpunished Crime*. He is not a scholarly authority on Lenin and knows about Lenin primarily through bitter personal experience. Still, Berzins' comment on Lenin's cynical game of international chess is fully in accord with the historical facts.

IN order to seize power, Lenin skillfully exploited the distrust and hatred between the Russian aristocracy, the bourgeoisie, the working classes and the impoverished peasantry. He managed to win the support of the masses of workers and peasants by promising bread to the hungry, peace to the weary and land to the landless.

However, the takeover in Petrograd, Moscow and the other major industrial centers was only the beginning of the consolidation of power in Russia. Before the final victory was to be achieved, Lenin and his group of revolutionaries had to fight on several fronts against intervention from abroad. What was worse, they also had to fight the enemies inside Russia—the "white" armies. . . .

Was it the genius of Lenin or an accident that finally ensured—against such odds and after years of desperate fighting—a bolshevik victory? Lenin himself offered an almost incontrovertible answer in his speech before the Conference of the Communist Party of the Moscow district on November 21, 1920:

There is no need to prove that the armed forces of the RSFSR are ten, even one hundred times weaker than those of the capital-

istic countries. For three long years units of the British, French and Japanese armies were stationed on Russian territory. There is not the slightest doubt that the allied forces were sufficiently strong to have defeated us within a matter of months or even of weeks, with only a minimum of effort. . . . If we were able to conquer the interventionists, then it was only because their interests divided them, but united us. In utilizing the discord of our opponents, we gained a breathing space.

Thus the miracle of the Russian revolution, according to Lenin himself, can largely be traced to the discord and lack of unity among the allies, the centrifugal forces of their opposing interests, and a grudging fear on the part of each one of them that the others might gain greater benefits or privileges. . . .

Lenin's diabolically cynical attitude towards the capitalists and the methods he advocated for dealing with them to the benefit of the communists, are as astonishing as is the frankness with which he discussed the matter.

* * *

Lenin's unpublished notes stated:

As a result of my own direct observations

From Alfreds Berzins, *The Two Faces of Co-existence* (New York: Robert Speller & Sons, 1967), pp. 6–8, 10–11, 15–16, 18–20, 22–23, 25–29, 31–35. Reprinted by permission of the publisher.

during my emigration, I must admit that the so-called cultured elements of Western Europe and America are incapable of comprehending the present state of affairs and the actual balance of forces; these elements must [be] regarded as deaf-mutes and treated accordingly. . . .

A revolution never develops along a direct line, by continuous expansion, but forms a chain of outbursts and withdrawals, attacks and lulls, during which the revolutionary forces gain strength in preparation for their final victory.

. . . in view of the protracted nature of the growth of the world socialist revolution, it is necessary to resort to special maneuvers capable of accelerating our victory over capitalist countries. We must:

a) In order to placate the deaf-mutes, proclaim the (fictional!) separation of our government and governmental institutions (the Council of People's Commissars, etc.) from the Party and Politburo and, in particular, from the Comintern, declaring these latter agencies to be independent political groups which are tolerated on the territory of the Soviet Socialist Republics. The deaf-mutes will believe it.

b) Express a desire for the immediate resumption of diplomatic relations with capitalist countries on the basis of complete non-interference in their internal affairs. Again the deaf-mutes will believe it. They will even be delighted and will fling wide open their doors, through which emissaries of the Comintern and Party intelligence agencies will quickly infiltrate into these countries disguised as our diplomatic, cultural and trade representatives.

Speaking the truth is a petty-bourgeois prejudice. A lie, on the other hand, is often justified by the end. Capitalists the world over, and their governments, will, in their desire to win the Soviet market, shut their eyes to the above-mentioned activities and will thus be turned into blind deaf-mutes. They will furnish credits, which will serve us as a means of supporting the Communist parties in their countries and, by supplying us with materials and techniques which are not available to us, will rebuild our war industry, which is essential for our future attacks on our suppliers. In other words, they will be laboring to prepare their own suicide.

* * *

Before Russia could be secured for communism, Russia would have to become economically strong and viable.

An economically powerful Russia would be able to set up an army, equipped with the latest weapons—a proletarian army —which would then be in a position to organize and support the communist movement throughout the world. Russia itself did not possess either modern machinery or the specialists required to produce it, nor even the gold or currency with which to purchase the necessary machinery and equipment. It was imperative that the assistance of the capitalists be secured in some other way: the capitalists' greed for profit had to be aroused so that they would forget for a time their aversion to communist ideology and methods. That was Lenin's philosophy of action. He proposed to achieve this goal by offering concessions to the capitalists, even if this meant letting them have the lion's share of the gains for a while. . . .

However, Lenin saw still other advantages in granting concessions to the capitalists. He figured that if foreign capital were invested in Russia, armed intervention on the part of the capitalist countries would become less likely, as this would mean the loss of their investments.

* * *

During the years of civil strife which followed the revolution, . . . industry . . . was in a state of complete collapse. There were shortages of parts for imported machinery and shortages of trained engineers and technicians. These had either fled to the West or fallen victim to the Cheka terror. . . . Only about one-tenth of the pre-war industrial plant and equipment was operational in 1920.

How to overcome these difficulties? The granting of concessions promised some measure of relief. But concessions alone could not attract sufficient credit for the purchase of new plant and equipment on a large scale and within the time required. To supplement this, Lenin considered a propaganda campaign with appropriate slogans. The nations of Europe had not as yet recovered from the horrors and misery of the First World War. For this reason Lenin selected the slogan "For peace and economic prosperity!" while promising at the same time the widest and most whole-hearted support of the Soviet Union. His reasoning was that, in the event of a hesitation on the part of the capitalists to cooperate with the Soviet government in the economic sphere (either out of a hatred for communism or a dislike of their methods of nationalization and suppression), such a propaganda campaign might induce the anti-capitalist classes to exert pressure on their governments. According to Lenin, economic co-operation could be considered not only an economic, but also a political victory for the Soviet Union.

* `* *

Among the more important promises of a political nature which Lenin made at that time was the assurance of peaceful coexistence among nations with differing political systems and the promise of non-interference by the communists in the internal affairs of other countries. What would have been the implications of such promises had they been strictly followed? Adherence to these principles would have implied no less than a renunciation of the goal of world revolution. It would have meant . . . the voluntary renunciation of Marx's and Lenin's goal of a classless society extending across the face of the earth, unfettered by the boundaries of nationality or state. For these reasons, Lenin was never further from the truth than when he promised peaceful co-existence to Europe, Japan and the United States of America. To Lenin co-existence was not an end but a means for gaining time. He hoped to use this time to strengthen and re-align his forces so that they would be ready for attack whenever and wherever some weakness began to show in the capitalist system. . . .

Again and again Lenin advised his followers not to be afraid of concessions and of co-existence. He reminded them that during the civil war the capitalist countries had such an overwhelming advantage in terms of weapons and men that it should have taken only the slightest effort on their part to defeat the communists in Russia. In spite of this communism emerged victorious. And the same, he predicted, would happen also in the new battles being drawn up on the economic front. Lenin felt that by learning from the capitalists, with their own aid and assistance, the most up to date methods of production, and by establishing modern factories, a solid economic base would be created in less developed areas.

We get tremendous economic benefit from concessions. . . . This is also a kind of war . . . . But this war is advantageous to us in all respects, and the transition from the old war to the new is also advantageous, not to speak of the fact that there is a certain indirect guarantee of peace. I said at the meeting, that we have just now passed from war to peace, but we have not forgotten that war will return. So long as capitalism and socialism remain, they cannot live at peace. In the long run one or the other will be victorious, the funeral dirge will be sounded either over the Soviet Republic or over world capitalism.

Concessions and the prospects of handsome profits offered by the Soviet Union eventually did manage to arouse the interest—and greed—of certain businessmen in the capitalistic world. With their aid the Soviets acquired the necessary industrial plant and equipment, the railway rolling stock and the technical advisers they needed. Politically, however, the Soviet Union remained isolated. . . .

In the spring of 1919 the Soviet Government was groping for indirect contacts that would lead to the commencement of peace negotiations with the great powers of the west. On May 7, 1919, G. V. Chicherin, the then Commissar for Foreign Affairs . . . suggested that peace talks should be initiated, with the proviso that, simultaneously, there would be a complete cessation of all hostilities directed against the Soviet Union. . . .

If for no other reason than for its propaganda effect, Lenin repeated again and again his offer of peace to the Entente powers. . . .

One can assume that Lenin did not expect these efforts to be crowned with any real success. . . . But he could be sure that the propaganda value of these proposals would be significant, as there are always trusting souls all over the world who take the communist peace proposals at their face value and, for humanitarian or other reasons, take it upon themselves to popularize the propaganda slogans of the communists.

In his speech to the Seventh All-Russian Congress of Soviets on December 5, 1919, Lenin evaluated the propaganda value of the peace proposals as they affected the intellectuals in the free world.

Comrades, from what I have said, about our international successes it follows—and, I think, it is not necessary to dwell at length on this— that we must repeat our peace proposal in a manner that is calm and business-like to the maximum degree. We must do this because we have already made such a proposal many times. Each time we made this proposal, we gained something in the eyes of every educated man, even if he was our enemy. . . .

With the formation of the Comintern, Lenin had at his disposal small but well organized propaganda units in the Western democracies, which acted strictly in accordance with the directives emanating from Moscow. The expected results did not fail to materialize. On December 5, 1919, at the All-Russian Conference of Soviets, Lenin could report that the October 26 issue of the French Socialist paper *Humanité* published an article demanding non-intervention on the part of the French government in the internal affairs of the Soviet Union. The first signature attached to this article was that of Anatole France. This was followed by the signatures of seventy other well-known French bourgeois intellectuals. In the same speech Lenin also reported that Parisian workers had, as a result of the skillful use of the communist peace and co-operation slogans, reached the point where they would not allow anyone to voice an opinion that was adverse in any way to the Soviet Union.

Lenin expressed satisfaction that even in the United States the liberal elements of the bourgeoisie rejected the malicious accusations regarding the Cheka terror which had been directed against the Soviet Union. As an example he mentions an article by Stewart Chase, published in the July 25, 1919 issue of *The New Republic*, which reproaches the Allies (i.e., England, France and the United States) for not recognizing the Soviet Union because the communist regime in that country allegedly subjected its citizens to mass terror. In his defense of the methods used by the Cheka, Chase even goes so far as to compare it with the "Mannerheim terror" in Finland. . . . It does not appear to be difficult to discern a difference between the armed suppression of the rebellious elements during the course of the Finnish war of liberation, which elements, moreover, were foreign inspired, and the systematic mass terror directed against the citizens of the Soviet Union, quite frequently for no other reason than that they had previously belonged to the well-to-do classes of society. Stewart Chase, however, was only one among many of the liberal-minded people of his time, as Lenin described them, who either could not, or would not, recognize this essential difference. Around the middle of February, 1920, a representative of the New York *Evening Journal* in Berlin obtained a radio interview with Lenin. Some of the answers are both interesting in themselves and characteristic of Lenin's political philosophy vis-à-vis the capitalists:

QUESTION: On what basis would it be possible to conclude a peace treaty with the United States of America?
LENIN'S ANSWER: Let the American capitalists leave us alone. We on our part will not attack them. We are even prepared to pay them in gold for the machinery, tools, etc., and our transportation systems.
QUESTION: What are the obstacles to this kind of peace?
LENIN'S ANSWER: None, on our part. What prevents a peace settlement is the imperialism of the Americans and other nations.
QUESTION: What is your opinion regarding the development of the Soviets as a real force throughout the world?

LENIN'S ANSWER: The future belongs to the Soviet system on a global scale. . . . Indeed, it could hardly be otherwise. If only the workers of the cities, the peasants and the artisans, along with the small landholders, in short, the vast majority of the workers, would correctly understand that the Soviet system puts all power into their hands, freeing them from the yoke of the landowners and capitalists, who would then be able to prevent the complete victory of the Soviet system throughout the world? . . .

QUESTION: Does Russia still fear the counter-revolution from abroad?

LENIN'S ANSWER: Regrettably, yes, as the capitalists are foolish people, greedy for materialistic things. They have already made several such foolish attempts, inspired by their cupidity. Therefore, there is reason to believe that they will repeat such attempts before the workers and peasants have succeeded in reeducating their capitalists.

QUESTION: Is Russia prepared to establish economic and trade relations with the United States?

LENIN'S ANSWER: Of course, we are prepared to do this, and, moreover, with all countries. The peace settlement with Estonia is surely proof that for the sake of establishing economic relations we are ready, under certain conditions, even to grant industrial concessions.

. . . During his long struggle for power, Lenin had learned to recognize fully the tremendous importance and power of propaganda. He therefore tried to use this tool on every suitable occasion.

. . . an important event in the foreign policy of the Soviet Union was the invitation to a conference on economic reconstruction in April of 1922, in Genoa, Italy. . . .

Because of the progressive worsening of his illness, Lenin was unable to attend the Genoa conference in person, but from his Moscow headquarters he supervised and practically conducted the entire work of the delegation. Immediately upon receipt of the invitation to participate in the Genoa conference, there began in Moscow a most careful preparation for the meetings. Detailed plans were worked out, outlining the most effective methods of sowing discord among the Entente powers and at the same time gaining a propaganda victory, thus forcing the leaders of the western great powers to pay close attention to Soviet demands in the future, because of the pressure of public opinion in their own countries favorable to the Soviet position.

It seems Lenin was convinced that the great capitalist powers of the west were bound to come out losers the moment they sat down at the same conference table with the new type of Soviet diplomatist. In Lenin's view the propositions advanced by the communists would have a strong advantage merely because the communists would be free to make full and liberal use of slogans which were popular among wide segments of the peoples of the entire world. For instance, General disarmament; Peace among nations; Co-existence between different political systems; Social rights for workers, etc. Into each of these slogans the Soviet diplomats would be able to insert the particular kind of meaning that would afford the greatest measure of success and advantage to the ideological expansion of communism.

In discussing the composition of the delegation and its aims and duties, before the International Peace Conference in the Hague in December 1922, which was convened at the initiative of the Amsterdam International of Trade Unions, Lenin advocated the selection of particularly good speakers. If, he said, it should not be possible for the Soviet delegation to deliver their propaganda speeches in full, they should use every guile at least to read into the conference record their theses which could then be suitably expanded and published in propaganda brochures.

In spite of the fact that in his March 6, 1922 speech Lenin asserted that the Soviet delegation would go to Genoa in the role of merchants and traders, little if anything relating to economic affairs is to be found in the work programme prepared by Chicherin prior to the conference, or in Lenin's own instructions to the delegates. In a letter dated March 10, 1922, Chicherin, who because of Lenin's illness had been appointed to lead the delegation, explains the main points of his work programme to Lenin, asking at the same time for more detailed instructions. In this letter Chicherin proposes that it would be advisable to concentrate in Genoa, in the first instance, on a "broad pacifist programme." That, he felt, ought to be the most important weapon in the arsenal of Soviet propaganda. . . . Further, Chicherin proposed a few innovations, which he felt would be useful at international conferences, as they might hinder the capitalists from using such conferences for their own ends. Among such innovations might be (1) to invite to international conferences (with equal rights) colonial nations, with the stipulation that the European powers are not to intervene in their internal affairs; (2) request that in the future, European international conferences should admit trade union representatives, with full voting privileges, on the condition that of each delegation at least one third should be representatives of workers' organizations. Chicherin felt that such a proposal by the Soviet Union would be extremely popular with the workers, [and] . . . would open the way to future battles, and strengthen the position of the Soviet Union against the imperialists. This type of organization, in its practical work, would be split into technical committees which could then defend the proposals put forward by the Soviet Union in regard to the reconstruction of the world and demand that the stronger give economic assistance to the weaker without exercising any domination over them. . . . After having acquainted himself with the 13 points of the tactical procedures outlined for the Soviet delegation for the Genoa economic conference by Chicherin, Lenin gave it general approval in a letter dated March 14, 1922. The full text of this letter is given below. . . . Lenin also made some additional suggestions. . . .

LETTER FROM V. I. LENIN TO
G. V. CHICHERIN

March 14, 1922

Comrade Chicherin,

I have read your letter of March 10. It seems to me that you have yourself outlined the pacifist programme excellently in that letter.

The great thing is to pronounce both the programme and our commercial proposals clearly and loudly *before* the break-up (if "they" make for an early break-up).

You and our delegation have the skill to do this.

In my opinion you already have about thirteen points (I am sending my marginal notes to your letter); they are excellent.

Everyone will be intrigued when we say: "We have an extensive and complete programme!" If they do not let us announce it we shall print it with a protest.

Everywhere there is a "tiny" proviso: we, the Communists, be it known, have *our own* communist programme (Third International) *but* deem it our duty as *merchants to support* (even if there is only one chance in ten thousand) the *pacifists in the other*, i.e., the bourgeois, camp (considering the Second and the Two-and-a-Half Internationals as belonging to that camp).

That will be venomous and "benign" and will help demoralise the enemy.

Using these tactics, we shall win *even* if we are unsuccessful at Genoa. We *shall not* make a deal that is not to our advantage.

With communist greetings,

Yours,

Lenin

March 14.

P.S.

Comrade Chicherin,

Why should we not be venomous (and "benign") in another way as well?

By proposing an abolition of all war debts (§14) and a *re-examination* (on the basis of our thirteen points) of the Versailles and *all* war treaties (§ 15), not by suppressing the minority by the voting power of the majority, but on the basis of *concord*, because we, present *here* in the capacity of merchants, *cannot put* forward *here* any other principle than that of commerce. We do not want to secure a majority vote over the United States; we are merchants and want *to persuade* that country!! Let the question be put to *all* countries and *make an attempt to persuade* those that are not in agreement. Benign and unacceptable to the bourgeoisie. We shall disgrace them and humiliate them "in a benign manner".

Variation: the subordination of the minority of countries (by population) to the majority may be proposed *separately* inside each of the two camps, bourgeois and Soviet (that which recognises private property and that which does not).

Put forward both the project and the variation.

Les rieurs seront avec nous!*

* The laughers will be on our side.

This letter of Lenin's to Chicherin is a classical example of all future diplomatic activity of Soviet delegations at later international conferences: "That will be venomous and 'benign' and will help to demoralize the enemy."

John Keep

MASTER TACTICIAN OF THE REVOLUTION

John Keep is Reader in Russian Studies at the School of Slavonic and East European Studies at the University of London. He has visited the Soviet Union several times for research and study and has done excellent work on various aspects of the revolutions of 1905 and 1917. He is the author of *Contemporary History in the Soviet Mirror* and *The Rise of Social Democracy in Russia,* the latter book providing a detailed commentary on almost every step and misstep in the trial-and-error evolution of Lenin as a politician through 1905. The following excerpt from one of his articles displays a similar gift for reasoned argument, based upon a detached view of Lenin's career. The very means that served Lenin so well in gaining and consolidating power, Keep concludes, failed miserably when applied to the tasks of governing.

LENIN'S "OPERATIONAL CODE"

IT must be emphasised that Lenin's ideas on tactics did not develop in a vacuum, from pure intellectual effort, but were a logical corollary of the "organisational plan" which he outlined as early as 1902, and to which he adhered even when the scale of his operations was incomparably greater. Lenin was remarkably consistent. He seldom modified his ideas in the light of experience; on the contrary, as his self-confidence grew, he increasingly referred back to his earlier conduct as a guide to the problems of the present. He sought to apply the same formula towards a handful of émigré comrades as he did later towards various segments of the Soviet population or the massed forces of "world imperialism."

Although Lenin's "operational code" is basically very simple and has often been described, it is perhaps worth while outlining the principal ideas here. The underlying notion is best conveyed by the phrase *divide et impera.* According to the original model, the active catalyst of change is a body of professional revolutionaries, bound together by close ties of loyalty to their leader, so homogeneous as to reduce to a minimum the likelihood of dissent or indiscipline. This central nucleus has divisions of function, but no formal or institutional barriers within it which could prevent the leader from exercising overall control—for example, by turning to the rank and file for support against errant colleagues at the top. A formal barrier does, however, exist between the members of this "hard core" organisation and those in its "soft" peripheral bodies, and the relationship between the two echelons is closely prescribed. The "front organisations" (to use the term that has since entered the language) are to enjoy formal autonomy, so that they may attract the broadest possible membership, but their activities are to be controlled by agents of the parent body, whose identity and purposes may well be concealed from their fellows. Leadership is provided by means of periodical political campaigns, devised by the central organisation and embodied in simple slogans that can readily be assimilated. Such campaigns serve a dual purpose: they enable certain limited goals to be attained, thus bring-

From John Keep, "Lenin as Tactician," *Lenin, the Man, the Theorist, the Leader: A Reappraisal,* ed. Leonard Schapiro and Peter Reddaway (New York: Frederick A. Praeger, 1968), pp. 140–157. Reprinted by permission of Frederick A. Praeger, Inc., Publishers, Pall Mall Press Ltd., and the Hoover Institution.

ing nearer the achievement of the ultimate ends of the movement; more important, they focus the loyalty of those
in the periphery and cause schisms in
the opposing forces (which, it is assumed, are organised on a similar pattern). Since the immediate, provisional
objectives seem relatively innocuous,
some elements in the adversary's camp
can be won over; further campaigns can
then be launched to strengthen their
new loyalties and win still more adher-
ents, who will naturally tend to rally to
the stronger side. Considerations of expediency alone dictate the speed of the
process whereby these vacillating elements are successively divorced from
their core organisation, neutralised,
brought under control, and finally absorbed. The object is to bring about a
situation in which one's embattled adversary, much reduced in numbers,
faces a solid phalanx of loyal troops and
either surrenders or is overwhelmed,
whereupon the Hegelian synthesis is
finally achieved.

The actual tactical doctrines asso-
ciated with this model of conflict resolution do not amount to much more than a
few common-sense rules and precepts.

The first of these rules is that unswerving dedication to the final aim must be
combined with extreme flexibility in the
choice of means. The tactical line may
have to be changed very suddenly when
new opportunities appear. The ultimate
ends of the movement are certainties
that cannot be questioned, but the immediate objectives, which depend partly
on the situation of the moment, are open
to discussion. In coming to a decision,
long-term and short-term goals have to
be balanced against each other. Too
much emphasis on the former leads to
the error of "dogmatism," and on the latter to that of "opportunism." The good
bolshevik takes account of environ-
mental factors, but only up to a certain
point, beyond which lies the slough of
khvostizm (literally, "tail-end-ism," or
lagging behind events). He should not
allow his actions to be dominated by external ("objective") circumstances, but
should seek to mould reality according
to his will. His motto should be "courage,

courage, yet more courage"—here Lenin
is citing Marx, who in turn is citing Dan-
ton. Yet one should not allow one's enthusiasm to run away with one, for this
leads to the opposite error of "subjectivism." A leader who becomes isolated
from the masses, who confuses his own
false image of reality with the actual
substance, will lead the party into adven-
tures—actions for which the conditions have not matured and which are
therefore foredoomed to failure. The
ideal posture is a blend of determinism
and voluntarism, with a strong bias towards the latter.

The second rule relates to the different techniques required in offence and
defence. When conditions are favourable, the attack must be pressed home
relentlessly, with no slackening of impetus; all opportunities must be seized
boldly, so that the party's route to its
objectives may be as short and direct as
possible. On the other hand, when the
enemy is attacking, the correct tactic is
to retreat in good order, regroup one's
forces, and prepare for the inevitable
turn of the tide; it is necessary to manoeuvre and temporise, distract the enemy's attention by feints, giving way neither to panic nor to romantic illusions
about the chances of victory. Above all,
one should be realistic. "If you can't ad-
just yourself, if you won't crawl on your
belly in the mud, then you're not a revolutionary but a chatterbox," as Lenin
put it pithily to the delegates at the Seventh Party Congress in March 1918. A
few weeks later, addressing the All-Russian Central Executive Committee of the
Soviets, he claimed that from recent experience the bolsheviks had learned that
"one has to follow a tactic of relentless
pressure when objective conditions permit this, when . . . the masses are
aroused. But we have to resort to wait-
and-see tactics, to a slow accumulation
of forces, when objective conditions do
not allow a summons to general merciless resistance."

From these directives it follows that
no single mode of action can be considered valid in all circumstances, and that
most situations demand a combination
of several. It would be wrong, for exam-

ple, either to exaggerate or to minimise the value of legal as against clandestine activity or of peaceful propaganda as against violence. These are not antithetical but complementary, and it is up to the decision-maker to opt for the right balance between the various courses of action open to him. In other words, he is faced with the problem of ordering his priorities.

One has to be able at each moment to find that particular link in the chain which, if one grasps it with all one's might, will give one a firm grip upon the whole chain and a solid basis from which to go on to the next link—remembering that the order of the links, their interconnection, their distinctions, are not so simple and straightforward in a historical setting as they are in the blacksmith's shop.

The theory of the "decisive link" was much esteemed by Stalin and was partly responsible for the view, tenaciously held by some Soviet officials, that government should be carried on by a series of offensive campaigns.

The fourth rule, or group of rules, concerns the compromises, agreements and alliances which the party, as one pole in the dialectical contradiction, has to make with the vacillating elements that drift into its orbit during the course of the conflict. As early as 1899 Lenin remarked to a colleague about the Russian liberals: "I think that 'to utilise' is a much more accurate and appropriate word than 'to support' or 'to ally with,' which give the impression of equality, whereas they ought to follow along in the rear with clenched teeth." As he saw it, such partnerships were inherently unstable since they were based upon a transient community of interests. Once the joint adversary had been defeated—indeed, even some time before—the ally would begin to turn away unless forcibly prevented from doing so. For this reason the party must at all costs preserve its separate identity and its cohesion throughout the manoeuvre, lest it succumb to an act of treachery, and break off contact at exactly the correct moment for an initiative favourable to the party. The extent of the collaboration must de-

pend on the relative strength of those involved: the more powerful and united the core organisation, the greater the risks it could afford to take.

Lenin frequently inveighed against those idealistic but naive bolsheviks who failed to appreciate the need for such twists and turns of policy, although he did not face up squarely to the essentially moral nature of their criticism, and depicted them simply as "anarchists" deficient in tactical judgement. "The task of a revolutionary party," he explained in September 1917, "is not to renounce compromises altogether but to be able to remain loyal to its principles during all the compromises that may be necessary." Three years later he was preaching the same lesson to foreign sympathisers: "The whole history of bolshevism, before and after the October Revolution, is *full* of instances of manoeuvring [*lavirovanie*], agreements and compromises with others." Would one climb a mountain by the direct vertical route in preference to a zigzag path? Changing his metaphor, he went on to misquote Chernyshevsky: "Political activity is not like the Nevsky Prospekt." The error is not without interest; the economic determinist of the 1860s had contrasted the straight St. Petersburg avenue with the deviousness of history, whereas for the voluntarist Lenin it was political activity that mattered most. One had, said Lenin, to ensure that any such detour or compromise "does not lower but raises the general level of proletarian revolutionary consciousness"—i.e., strengthens the party's power position.

On inspection, Lenin's tactical doctrine boils down to little more than a series of injunctions to step forth boldly, stay alert, and keep one's powder dry. While it was sound enough so far as it went, it left a great deal unanswered. The most pertinent question was how these algebraic formulae were to be expressed in arithmetical terms, how they were to be quantified. How could one know when the moment had come to break an alliance or to pass over to more offensive methods? The stock answer was that this was determined by expediency. But this only left another unsolved question: who decides whether the results justify the action taken or not?

One is thus immediately thrown back to problems of organisation. In a party that identified itself with the onward march of history, only the leader could decide how far its actions were "correct." His was the aweful responsibility which the Hegelian could conveniently leave to the Godhead. And to make matters more difficult, this function could not be explicitly acknowledged, at least in Lenin's lifetime, since some pretence of collective rational decision-making had to be maintained; it was left to Stalin to claim powers of omniscience. Lenin was of necessity more modest, although even he made some extravagant assertions on behalf of his own proficiency as leader. "The art of the politician. . .," he wrote in *Left-wing Communism: an Infantile Disorder* (1920), "is to calculate correctly the conditions and moment in which the proletarian vanguard can successfully seize power, when it can subsequently win enough support from sufficiently wide segments of the working class, and when it can subsequently . . . extend and consolidate its rule, educating and teaching and attracting ever broader masses of working people. It is clear from the context that he is referring to his own experience in the Revolution. A little later in the same work, discussing the difference between "opportunistic" compromises and those that are permissible, he first says that "every worker understands the difference," but then concedes that it was often as hard to make out as the distinction between murder and homicide, and concludes: "One has to have one's head screwed on straight [*imet' sobstvennuyu golovu na plechakh*]to know what to do in each case. That, by the way, is why we have party organisations and party leaders deserving of the name, [who can] develop the necessary knowledge and experience, the necessary political flair to decide complex political questions quickly and correctly." But this was not very different from the theory propounded by the "idealist" Clausewitz, who affirmed his belief in *der Blitz des Geistes*—that flash of spiritual lightning which illumined the intellect of a successful commander in the heat of battle, the unconscious impulse which enabled him to surmount unexpected difficulties. When Lenin read this passage, he underlined it three times and noted: "Truth is not in systems." Not book learning but the power of judgement acquired from experience in action—this was the prerequisite of successful leadership. Or, to put it another way, what is today sometimes called "the *x* factor," the unpredictable subjective or chance element, could on occasion make all the difference between victory and defeat.

This was indeed a valuable insight, but it was difficult to reconcile with conventional Marxist determinism, and could not very well be developed at length in public. Instead, a host of devious arguments, and where necessary measures of physical coercion, had to be employed to conceal the fact that the party's supposedly "scientific" tactics were as often as not decided very arbitrarily, by the spiritual enlightenment of its leader. The most obvious of these devices was to emit a cloud of accusations against those previously identified with the course that it was now found expedient to reject, while simultaneously denying that any significant change had taken place. Thus, in the early months of 1918 the left-wing communists were roundly upbraided as "utopians" and "schismatics" for advocating the revolutionary guerrilla war against the invader to which Lenin had committed himself before the bolshevik seizure of power. Another ruse was to reinterpret earlier statements or formulas in a sense contrary to that given them at the time—a task much eased by the abstract and vague phraseology of Marxism. The term "democratic revolution," for example, did not mean in 1917 what it had signified in 1905. Nor did Lenin find it convenient to spell out in full the implications of his tactical line where to do so might have brought his party into discredit. It is also true that the blinkering effect of Marxist doctrine often hindered him from appreciating all the likely consequences of his actions, and he was liable to ignore whatever did not easily fit into his restricted view of human nature and behaviour. When unforeseen effects of his policies obliged him to take remedial action, he seldom acknowledged that the original decision had been at fault, and his first impulse was usually to cast about for a suitable scapegoat. A readiness to employ devious measures of this kind was not original or exclusive to Lenin, and may even be characteristic of the species *homo politicus;* nevertheless, taken in conjunction with his boundless ambitions and addiction to violence, it gave his teaching a markedly sinister quality.

THE CODE IN ACTION

A thorough study of Lenin's successes and failures as leader of the Bolshevik Party and Soviet state would require a full-scale biography, since virtually every step he took was motivated at least in part by the hope of tactical gain. We may confine ourselves to examining two episodes from the earlier part of his career and then consider the key period in his life when his skilful handling of affairs stands out in high relief.

The first example seems to show Lenin erring in the direction of excessive voluntarism. At the Second Congress of the RSDWP [Russian Social Democratic Workers' Party] in 1903, evidently overestimating the extent of his support within the party, he pushed through his own scheme for its reorganisation with such ruthlessness as to provoke a schism. He had expected that the democratic elements, discredited by his propaganda in *Iskra* as "economists," "opportunists," "revisionists," and the like, would be utterly routed, and that his uneasy colleagues on the editorial board of *Iskra* would bow to his will by helping him build a centralised, disciplined organisation under his own active leadership. These calculations proved to be mistaken; his fellow editors revolted against his high-handed methods and within a year he had lost all his positions of authority within the party. The schism had the important effect of paralysing Russian social democracy at the very moment when, with the outbreak of war in the Far East, great revolutionary opportunities were opening

up before it. For this reason not only the mensheviks but also many of Lenin's own associates condemned his line as unduly "sectarian." But he refused to accept any responsibility for the split, laid the blame wholly upon his opponents, and called on the rank and file to assist in building up a "true" party in place of the existing one, which had been sullied by treachery. Lenin's argument was that "all the organs of the party are conspiring against the party." The implication was that only he and his followers represented its real "consciousness," its revolutionary self, and that all means were justified in ridding it of its temporary heterodox leadership.

One might have expected that this hysterical argument, with its overtones of some medieval religious disputation, would have been treated with contempt; but the intellectual climate in the party was not conducive to precise or rational thought, and extravagant accusations were readily believed. It was widely assumed that the very vehemence with which Lenin presented his grievances indicated that he must have had at least some right on his side. In the event, many of his critics were willing to give him the benefit of the doubt and to make concessions in the hope of securing a lasting compromise. This was eventually accomplished in 1906, whereupon Lenin was restored, temporarily at least, to a position of eminence. While in a sense his intransigence had paid dividends, one may doubt whether the struggle was worth while even from a narrow Leninist point of view. There is much evidence to suggest that, if the bolsheviks had adopted a more sophisticated, permissive approach, they might have wielded greater influence in the party and in radical circles generally during the Revolution of 1905–7 than they actually did.

In the broader arena, however, Lenin does seem to have become more flexible and venturesome after 1905. This was partly due to the conviction, based on experience, that some "open" organisations could serve a useful purpose as media for the mobilisation of public opinion. This did not imply any concession to constitutionalism, any willingness to allow himself to be influenced by the ideas which others might express in debate. Rather the reverse: he was less fearful than before of enemy penetration, provided the necessary safeguards were taken, and more confident that bolshevism could compete effectively in the political market-place. For this reason he advocated participation in the first Duma. He argued in favour of this course as early as December 1905, at the Tammerfors conference, but then yielded to the left-wing activists who dominated the proceedings, and whom he could ill afford to affront after the disastrous Moscow uprising. These enthusiasts, strangers to the dialectic, were opposed on principle to participation in a parliamentary-type assembly. Convinced that a new revolutionary upsurge was in the offing, they stood by the old insurrectionary tactics. For the next few months Lenin publicly endorsed this idea, although it is difficult to say how far the wish was father to the thought.

Eventually his sense of realism gained the upper hand. As the summer of 1906 wore on, with only limited manifestations of popular discontent, he changed his line. In July he advocated guerrilla action rather than insurgency on the 1905 pattern; in August he startled his colleagues by advising them to participate in the elections to the second Duma. Lest his prestige suffer by the sudden shift, he continued to maintain that his earlier tactical line, involving a boycott of the Duma, had been correct, and when recalcitrant leftists charged him with inconsistency, replied with counter-accusations of "dogmatism," "anarchism," and other sins. He also claimed that there was a substantial difference between his own position and that of the mensheviks, who had advocated participation in the elections to the first Duma as well as in those to the second. The argument was not very plausible, but it was politically astute. Not until fourteen years later, when memories of the affair had dimmed and he was anxious to overcome left wing extremism in the Comintern, did he admit that the initial boycott of the Duma had been mistaken. Even so, he did not ac-

knowledge that his policy had vacillated under contrary pressures from the left and from the right.

By 1917, we are confronted by a Lenin more self-confident than ever of his manipulative skill, heartened as well as embittered by the war. He is of course greatly helped by the fluidity of Russian politics after the overthrow of the tsar, which ensures that such errors of judgement as he makes are generally outweighed by those of his adversaries. No sooner has he returned to Petrograd than he propounds the startling doctrine that the bourgeois phase of revolution, although barely a few weeks old, has already exhausted its potentialities, and that power must pass to the proletariat and its allies. A Soviet régime is to overthrow the bourgeoisie, end the war, and set the scene for the international socialist revolution. This is no mere tactical shift but a revision of basic strategy: strong medicine for those party stalwarts who had read Marx but never really understood Lenin. As they listened to his exposition, Sukhanov tells us, "their eyes roved about unseeingly, showing complete confusion." Yet within a month he has brought them round to his point of view, not by convincing them that his opinions are ideologically sound, but by employing "organisational" methods. He communicates directly with the rank and file, who respond readily to the new gospel, and the activists and generals must either rally to him or forfeit their authority.

At the same time Lenin is careful not to identify himself too closely with the semi-anarchistic masses who flock to his banner and, by trying to force the pace, implicitly challenge his leadership. He preserves his control by giving tacit encouragement to the participants in the demonstrations against Milyukov, but then lightly reprimands them for premature use of the slogan "All Power to the Soviets!"—premature because he had recommended "patient systematic explanatory work" by the bolsheviks to win a majority in the soviets before they took power. Outwardly he appears to preach restraint to the war-weary masses; but this leaves him wholly free to scourge the government for its pusillanimity in dealing with the urgent issues of the day and to build up his party's organisational strength. In the "June Days" his forces pass in review, as it were; while the majority socialists win a formal victory, the events in the streets show that the bolsheviks are increasing their hold. New slogans are conjured forth from the Kshesinskaya Palace* to maintain the momentum of advance. Yet the front is somewhat ragged; it is open to argument whether Lenin really sought to provoke a confrontation with the Soviet by his forceful statement on June 3 that his party was willing to take power, or whether it was an ill-judged gesture which turned moderate opinion against him.

It was his good fortune that any effect this might have had was nullified by the controversy aroused by Kerensky's ill-fated offensive. Lenin is thus able to parry the blow. But events then move too fast for him. In the "July days" he vacillates, anxious to exploit the crowd's discontent yet fearful that this is not yet the moment for general insurrection. The fiasco undermines his standing in the party: on the right wing he is regarded as irresponsible, on the left as inconsistent. It is a bad moment for Lenin, and it is not surprising that in the Finnish marshes he should over-react to the bolshevik defeat. He announces that the counter-revolution has triumphed and repudiates the slogan of "All Power to the Soviets!"; the party itself is to carry out the insurrection, but this is seen as a fairly distant objective. The proceedings of the Sixth Congress indicate that, as on so many other occasions, his lieutenants fail to appreciate the finer implications of this tactical shift and continue to regard the soviets as organs of insurrection, adhering to the line which had been set in April. Perhaps the difference between their position and his own might have assumed more importance had he remained in Petrograd, or had the pace of events been less hectic; but as it happened he is saved by the Kornilov affair.

* Bolshevik headquarters in Petrograd. [Editor's note.]

This gives him the chance to outbid the left-wing extremists by adopting an ultra-radical stance and urging immediate preparations for insurrection. As in April, he wins over his party by a combination of pressure from above and from below. Announcing this new "revision of tactics," he is clearly on the defensive against the charge of "opportunism," but argues that this can be avoided by a campaign on two fronts: against Kerensky as well as Kornilov. This operation the bolsheviks and their allies now carry out with great dexterity, until the Provisional Government is isolated and discredited—a classic instance of the practical implementation of Lenin's teaching on alliances, since few members of the "Committee for Struggle against Counter-Revolution," created and effectively controlled by the bolsheviks, fully appreciate the part they are playing in the unfolding of Lenin's plans. His tactics achieve success because they are attuned to the "objective" situation, although not quite in the way that bolshevik spokesmen maintain. It is less a matter of mobilising "class-conscious proletarians" than of harnessing elemental energies and hatreds in all segments of society. In any case, there can be no doubt that the necessary work of "disinformation" by slogan and rumour is adroitly managed, and the very decisiveness of the October victory may be held to settle any argument about the correctness of his tactical line. Nevertheless, in the interests of historical accuracy, it is worth pointing out that Lenin was less astute than Trotsky in his appreciation of the role which various mass bodies could play in the organisation of the coup. Thus, participation in the "Pre-parliament" was not the risky venture that Lenin feared it to be, and the Second Congress of Soviets helped to disguise and legitimise the seizure of power. On these issues Lenin was the prisoner of his own recently adopted ultra-leftism; and if this caused him no serious damage, the credit lay primarily with his adversaries, whose errors of judgement far transcended his own.

The next few months show Lenin at the acme of his tactical skill. His success in consolidating his party's power was due to clever political manipulation rather than to use of the coercive instruments available to the ruling group. The latter were admittedly important, but they could not by themselves have turned the scales. In many of his key decisions at this time Lenin showed a masterly comprehension of political realities: for example, in his handling of the left socialist revolutionaries, whom he first excluded from his government, then admitted to play a decorative role, and finally allowed to depart once they had served their purpose. His treatment of the Constituent Assembly, symbol of the democratic opposition to bolshevism, showed an almost diabolical finesse: he resisted his initial inclination to prohibit it from convening at all, then progressively curtailed its scope for action, and at the crucial moment dissolved it without giving the deputies the chance of martyrdom or of effective resistance. Similarly, Lenin won over the peasants with the Land Decree, neutralised the national minorities by an apparently contradictory policy of concessions and coercion, and abandoned old slogans and commitments without compunction. At this period he was concerned solely with the preservation of his party in power, and for the sake of this he was willing to make virtually any manoeuvre that expediency might dictate. From his own point of view, which gave primacy to the political struggle, he was of course being perfectly consistent. Only Lenin was capable of such iron logic: certainly not Trotsky, who vacillated at Brest-Litovsk, or Stalin, who vacillated over the confrontation with the Constituent Assembly, and still less the left-wing communists with their high-minded but naive addiction to principle.

In this way Lenin secures his precious "breathing-space" and bolshevism survives. But, as the months pass by, history takes its revenge upon the great tactician; the problems which he has put off by skilful manoeuvring come relentlessly to the fore. Henceforth he finds himself increasingly on the defensive against forces whose raison d'être he does not understand, because there is no place for them in his narrow world-view.

HISTORY TAKES REVENGE

The bitter truth was that Lenin knew how to win power but not how to use it. This deficiency became painfully clear as the "international proletarian revolution," whose outbreak he had so confidently anticipated, failed to materialise, and his party faced the task of governing a people largely indifferent, if not hostile, to the ideas that animated their new rulers. Rather incautiously, perhaps, Lenin had committed to paper his views on the government of a socialist state; but these notions, borrowed by way of Marx from the nineteenth-century utopians, were soon proved totally irrelevant. Although it was possible to abandon them in practice, it was extremely difficult for him to evolve any new formulas to put in their place. Since *State and Revolution* could not be expunged from the Leninist canon, the bolsheviks had to maintain that its principles were being applied in real life and to make belief in this fiction obligatory upon all Soviet citizens. Thus Lenin's Russia became the world's first, albeit rather imperfect, totalitarian state: that is to say, a country in which the principal feature of public life was a sharp contrast between reality and its official image. The fraudulent element which thereby entered into the Soviet political order stemmed ultimately from Lenin's own manipulative approach, which he carried over mechanically into the post-revolutionary era. He tackled his work as ruler of Soviet Russia, as architect of the new régime, in precisely the same spirit as he had the struggle for power. He could not grasp that a sovereign state was essentially different from a revolutionary party, and that to attempt to run it by the same methods must lead to disaster, by destroying that mutual trust between rulers and ruled which is the basis of civilised government.

Until the day of his retirement from public affairs, Lenin continued to believe that laws and institutions had no real part to play in regulating the life of a socialist society, but should be eradicated along with other relics of the bourgeois state; that direct democracy by the working masses was both possible and reconcilable with single-party dictatorship; that the old informal camaraderie of the underground could be carried over into a governing party with hundreds of thousands of members; that moral exhortation and a good example at the top would suffice to keep all those in authority loyal, honest, efficient, responsible and humane in their attitude to the toiling poor. When all these ideas were shown to be utopian nonsense, Lenin could not take the necessary dialectical leap to a realm of higher truths; instead, he was left by the wayside of history, clinging pathetically to his timeworn theoretical baggage. On occasion he would utter an ineffectual protest at some retrograde phenomenon to which the Revolution had given rise; more frequently he would suppress his doubts and. assert that all was well. "I hate bureaucracy heartily; it paralyses and corrupts from above and from below," he says to Klara Zetkin; but the remedies he devises are often worse than the disease. In a régime that cries out for order and legality, his use of his old manipulative techniques merely adds to the prevailing chaos by confusing people's ideas about the purposes of the supreme power.

In November 1918, for example, Lenin "agitates" for a more conciliatory line towards the petty bourgeoisie (by which he understands the smaller property-owning peasants and the professional men). "Now that these people are beginning to turn towards us, we ought not to turn away from them just because we used to have a different slogan in our pamphlets; we ought to rewrite these pamphlets . . . and say that we're not afraid to use conciliation as well as coercion." But in the next breath he justifies as necessary the violence done to these peasants by the class struggle in the countryside, since "war is war"; he does not suggest any check upon the arbitrariness of the Cheka or other instruments of the dictatorship, the chief obstacle to any sincere collaboration on the part of the elements concerned. It might be argued that this apparent inconsistency on Lenin's part is deliberate, that he is trying to weaken and divide the opposing forces by holding out a carrot while applying the stick. This is partly so, but it would be wrong to go too far in rationalising his policy, to see in it a logic that is no longer there; rather might it be said that he is groping in the dark but failing to come up with answers to his problems. The same applies to his policy towards the national minorities. On countless occasions he urges his followers not to surrender to chauvinistic tendencies, and to heed the sensitivities of the non-Russian peoples, yet he simultaneously authorises acts of violence on their part which are bound to stimulate opposition and a desire for genuine national independence. This is not so much machiavellian tactics as an endeavour to reconcile the irreconcilable, to have both real federal equality and unlimited dictatorship. In effect, the Lenin of 1918–22 has no "nationalities policy" but flounders from one enforced expedient to the next.

Even the transition to the New Economic Policy, which is sometimes viewed almost as an act of statesmanship, seems in retrospect little more than another such expedient, hastily conceived under external pressure, which left open the major questions regarding its scope and duration. Only in one sphere were the decisions at the Tenth Congress clearly the fruit of calculation: in their effect upon the situation within the party itself. Here on this familiar territory Lenin preserves his old competence. He artfully discredits the leaders of the potentially popular Workers' Opposition as "anarcho-syndicalists," saddles Trotsky with the onus of identification with authoritarian policies, pushes through his own ostensibly "centrist" platform, which in effect subordinates the unions to the bureaucracy, and under the impact of the Kronstadt rising wins general support for a resolution making "factionalism" a punishable offence. A similar expertise is evident in his handling of Comintern politics, where he dexterously makes the unpopular Paul Levi the scapegoat for the failure of the attempted *putsch* in Germany of March 1921, so preserving the bolsheviks' image relatively untarnished and making it possible to go over to an effective "united front" strategy.

However, it soon emerged that the power-political thinking which Lenin had imposed on his party in Russia could not be transposed automatically to a foreign environment, where bolshevism was one of several competing currents, and disillusionment with its cynical practices was bound to find free expression. In Russia, on the other hand, the problem of widening the régime's popular base could be solved by forceful methods.

The party's problems were greatly eased by Lenin's withdrawal from the scene after 1922 and his eventual replacement by Stalin. No longer did its members need to wrestle with their consciences, as Lenin had done, to reconcile the requirements of practical politics with the overt goals of the Revolution; instead they could become straightforward functionaries, executives rather than decision-makers, who received their tactical line ready-made from above. They ceased to treat Lenin's ideas as a source of inspiration and were content to render them respectful but meaningless lip service. One of the many paradoxes of the Stalinist era was that, with the elimination of autonomous political forces from Soviet life, the principal sphere in which Lenin's manipulative tactics continued to be employed was within the party leadership itself—until the bizarre and horrific climax was reached with the purges of the late 1930s.

V. I. Lenin

ADVOCATE OF MANEUVER AND COMPROMISE

In 1920 Lenin was anxious to obtain a breathing spell in his war for world revolution, especially since he saw no signs of capitalism's imminent collapse. But Communists in Western Europe, desirous of emulating the Bolshevik success in Russia, had to be restrained lest they damage the cause needlessly by reckless ventures having no chances of victory. The result was Lenin's pamphlet *Left Wing Communism* directed against revolutionary immaturity. In this section of that book he berates the tactical folly of western Communists for not entering "reactionary" trade unions and "bourgeois" parliaments, if only to spread through them the gospel of the revolution. Lenin's followers, in aiming for tactical flexibility, have made political maneuver and compromise standard practices. Although Keep touches upon these methods in the preceding selection, Lenin's own words on the subject is essential reading.

WE cannot but regard as ridiculous and childish nonsense the pompous, very learned, and frightfully revolutionary disquisitions of the German Lefts to the effect that Communists cannot and should not work in reactionary trade unions, that it is permissible to turn down such work, that it is necessary to leave the trade unions and to create an absolutely brand-new, immaculate "Workers' Union" invented by very nice (and, probably, for the most part very youthful) Communists, etc., etc....

It is precisely this absurd "theory" that Communists must not work in reactionary trade unions that brings out with the greatest clarity how frivolous is the attitude of the "Left" Communists towards the question of influencing "the masses," and to what abuses they go in their vociferations about "the masses." If you want to help "the masses" and to win the sympathy and support of "the masses," you must not fear difficulties, you must not fear the pinpricks, chicanery, insults and persecution on the part of the "leaders" (who, being opportunists and social-chauvinists, are in most cases directly or indirectly connected with the bourgeoisie and the police), but must imperatively *work wherever the masses are to be found.* You must be capable of every sacrifice, of overcoming the greatest obstacles in order to carry on agitation and propaganda systematically, perseveringly, persistently and patiently, precisely in those institutions, societies and associations—even the most ultra-reactionary—in which proletarian or semi-proletarian masses are to be found. And the trade unions and workers' cooperatives (the latter sometimes, at least) are precisely organizations where the masses are to be found. According to figures quoted in the Swedish paper *Folkets Dagblad Politiken* on March 10, 1920, trade union membership in Great Britain increased from 5,500,000 at the end of 1917 to 6,600,000 at the end of 1918, an increase of 19 per cent. Towards the close of 1919 the membership was estimated at 7,500,000. I have not at hand the corresponding figures for France and Germany, but absolutely incontestable and generally known facts testify to a rapid growth of trade union membership in these countries too.

These facts make crystal clear what

From V. I. Lenin, *Selected Works*, Vol. II (Moscow: Foreign Languages Publishing House, 1951), pp. 359–360, 373, 377–378, 380–383, 395–398.

is confirmed by thousands of other symptoms, namely, that class consciousness and the desire for organization are growing precisely among the proletarian masses, among the "rank and file," among the backward elements. Millions of workers in Great Britain, France and Germany are·*for the first time* passing from a complete lack of organization to the elementary, lowest, most simple, and (for those still thoroughly imbued with bourgeois-democratic prejudices) most easily comprehensible form of organization, namely, the trade unions; yet the revolutionary, but imprudent, Left Communists stand by, shouting "the masses, the masses!"—and *refuse to work within the trade unions!!* refuse on the pretext that they are "reactionary"!! and invent a brand-new, immaculate little "Workers' Union," which is guiltless of bourgeois-democratic prejudices and innocent of craft or narrow craft-union sins, which, they claim, will be (will be!) a broad organization, and the only (only!) condition of membership of which will be "recognition of the Soviet system and the dictatorship!!"

Greater foolishness and greater damage to the revolution than that caused by the "Left" revolutionaries cannot be imagined! Why, if we in Russia today, after two and a half years of unprecedented victories over the bourgeoisie of Russia and the Entente, were to make "recognition of the dictatorship" a condition of trade union membership, we should be committing a folly, we should be damaging our influence over the masses, we should be helping the Mensheviks. For the whole task of the Communists is to be able to *convince* the backward elements, to work *among* them, and not to *fence themselves off* from them by artificial and childishly "Left" slogans. . . .

Should we participate in bourgeois parliaments?

The German "Left" Communists, with the greatest contempt—and with the greatest frivolity—reply to this question in the negative. Their arguments? In the passage quoted above we read: "One must emphatically reject . . . all reversion to parliamentary forms of struggle, which have become historically and politically obsolete."

Is parliamentarism "politically obsolete"? That is quite another matter. Were that true, the position of the "Lefts" would be a strong one. But it has to be proved by a most searching analysis, and the "Lefts" do not even know how to approach it. How can one say that "parliamentarism is politically obsolete," when "millions" and "legions" of *proletarians* are not only still in favour of parliamentarism in general, but are downright "counterrevolutionary"! Clearly, parliamentarism in Germany is *not yet* politically obsolete. Clearly, the "Lefts" in Germany have mistaken *their desire*, their political-ideological attitude, for objective reality. That is the most dangerous mistake for revolutionaries. . . . Parliamentarism, of course, is "politically obsolete" for the Communists in Germany; but—and that is the whole point—we must *not* regard what is obsolete *for us* as being obsolete *for the class*, as being obsolete *for the masses*. Here again we find that the "Lefts" do not know how to reason, do not know how to act as the party of the *class*, as the party of the *masses*. You must not sink to the level of the masses, to the level of the backward strata of the class. That is incontestable. You must tell them the bitter truth. You must call their bourgeois-democratic and parliamentary prejudices—prejudices. But at the same time you must *soberly* follow the *actual* state of class consciousness and preparedness of the whole class (not only of its Communist vanguard), of all the toiling *masses* (not only of their advanced elements).

Even if not "millions" and "legions," but only a fairly large *minority* of industrial workers follow the Catholic priests —and a similar minority of rural workers follow the landlords and kulaks (Grossbauern)—it *undoubtedly* follows that parliamentarism in Germany is *not yet* politically obsolete, that participation in parliamentary elections and in the struggle on the parliamentary rostrum is *obligatory* for the party of the revolutionary proletariat *precisely* for the purpose of educating the backward strata of *its own class*, precisely for the purpose of awakening and enlightening the undeveloped, downtrodden, ignorant rural *masses*. As long as you are unable to disperse the bourgeois parliament and every other type of reactionary institution, you *must* work inside them *precisely* because there you will still find workers who are doped by the priests and by the dreariness of rural life; otherwise you risk becoming mere babblers. . . .

"One must emphatically reject all compromise with other parties . . . all policy of manoeuvring and compromise," write the German Lefts in the Frankfurt pamphlet.

It is a wonder that, holding such views, these Lefts do not emphatically condemn Bolshevism! For the German Lefts must know that the whole history of Bolshevism, both before and after the October Revolution, is *full* of instances of manoeuvring, temporizing and compromising with other parties, bourgeois parties included!

To carry on a war for the overthrow of the international bourgeoisie, a war which is a hundred times more difficult, protracted and complicated than the most stubborn of ordinary wars between states, and to refuse beforehand to manoeuvre, to utilize the conflict of interests (even though temporary) among one's enemies, to refuse to temporize and compromise with possible (even though temporary, unstable, vacillating and conditional) allies— is not this ridiculous in the extreme? Is it not as though, when making a difficult ascent of an unexplored and heretofore inaccessible mountain, we were to refuse beforehand ever to move in zigzags, ever to retrace our steps, ever to abandon the course once selected and to try others? And yet we find that people so immature and inexperienced (if youth were the explanation, it would not be so bad; young people are ordained by god himself to talk such nonsense for a period) meet with the support —whether direct or indirect, open or covert, whole or partial, does not matter—of some members of the Communist Party of Holland!! . . . The more powerful enemy can be vanquished only by exerting the utmost effort, and *without fail*, most thoroughly, carefully, attentively and skillfully using every, even the smallest, "rift" among the enemies, of every antagonism of interest among the bourgeoisie of the various countries and among the various groups or types of bourgeoisie within the various countries, and also by taking advantage of every, even the smallest, opportunity of gaining a mass ally, even though this ally be temporary, vacillating, unstable, unreliable and conditional. Those who fail to understand this, fail to understand even a particle of Marxism, or of scientific, modern Socialism *in general*. Those who have not proved by *deeds* over a fairly considerable period of time, and in fairly varied political situations, their ability to apply this truth in practice have not yet learned to assist the revolutionary class in its struggle to emancipate all toiling humanity from the exploiters. . . .

The Russian revolutionary Social-Democrats repeatedly utilized the services of the bourgeois liberals prior to the downfall of tsardom, that is, they concluded numerous practical compromises with them; and in 1901–02, even prior to the appearance of Bolshevism, the old editorial board of *Iskra* (consisting of Plekhanov, Axelrod, Zasulich, Martov, Potresov and myself) concluded (not for long, it is true) a formal political alliance with Struve, the political leader of bourgeois liberalism, while at the same time it was able to wage an unremitting and most merciless ideological and political struggle against bourgeois liberalism and against the slightest manifestation of its influence in the working-class movement. The Bolsheviks have always adhered to this policy. Beginning with 1905, they have systematically advocated an alliance between the working class and the peasantry against the liberal bourgeoisie and tsardom, never, however, refusing to support the bourgeoisie against tsardom (for instance, during second rounds of elections, or during second ballots) and never ceasing their relentless ideological and political struggle against the bourgeois revolutionary peasant party, the "Socialist-Revolutionaries," exposing them as petty-bourgeois democrats who falsely described themselves as Socialists. During the Duma elections in 1907, the Bolsheviks for a brief period entered into a formal political bloc with the "Socialist-Revolutionaries." Between 1903 and 1912 there were periods of several years in which we were formally united with the Mensheviks in one Social-Democratic Party; but we *never* ceased our ideological and political struggle against them as opportunists and vehicles of bourgeois influence among the proletariat. During the war we concluded certain compromises with the "Kautskyites," with the Left Mensheviks (Martov)', and with a section of the "Socialist-Revolutionaries" (Chernov and Natanson); we were together with them at Zimmerwald and Kienthal and issued joint manifestoes; but we never ceased and never relaxed our ideological and political struggle against the "Kautskyites," Martov and Chernov (Natanson died in 1919 a "Revolutionary Communist" Narodnik, he was very close to and almost in agreement with us). At the very moment of the October Revolution we entered into an informal but very important (and very successful) political bloc with the petty-bourgeois peasantry by adopting the *Socialist-Revolutionary* agrarian program *in its entirety*, without a single alteration —that is, we effected an unquestionable compromise in order to prove to the peasants that we did not want to "steam-roller" them, but to reach agreement with them. At the same time we proposed (and soon after effected) a formal political bloc, including participation in the government, with the "Left Socialist-Revolutionaries," who dissolved this bloc after the conclusion of the Brest-Litovsk Peace and then, in July 1918, went to the length of armed rebellion, and subsequently of armed struggle, against us.

III. TECHNICIAN OF POWER

Adam B. Ulam

FOUNDER OF THE PARTY OF DISCIPLINE

Adam B. Ulam is Professor of Government at Harvard University and Research Fellow of the Russian Research Center there. Born in Poland, he came to the United States in 1938, going on to a brilliant career in Russian studies. His books include *Titoism and the Cominform* and *Expansion and Coexistence: The History of Soviet Foreign Policy, 1917– 1967*. The book from which this selection is drawn is generally considered to be the best of all the Lenin biographies to date. In designing the prototype of the political party that would wield power over those whom it recruited, Lenin, according to Ulam, was writing "a primer of politics for the twentieth century."

W HAT Is To Be Done? is . . . a theory and a panegyric in praise of *the Party*, something then a novelty in political literature. The past political theorists and prophets extolled and claimed political power on behalf of a king, church, class, or leader. As yet this party existed only in Lenin's mind. It was to be composed of professional revolutionaries, but it was not a mere conspiracy. It was to enlist intellectuals, indeed from among them were to be sought its leaders, but it was to avoid the intellectuals' vices of continuous doctrinal dispute, indecision, humanitarian scruples, and the like. It was to rely upon workers, but certainly the Party's aims transcended the petty interests of the working class in securing a better livelihood and conditions of work.

Lenin thought of himself and wrote as a humble disciple of Karl Marx. His orderly and prosaic mind would have rebelled at the idea that his vision of the Party was closer to that of a collective superhuman Nietzschean hero or some medieval order of chivalry than to that of a humdrum political association, which the Social Democratic Party was supposed to be. Years were to pass before a

French poet was to sing of "my beautiful Communist Party." Admission to it in Russia for long depended on purity of (that is, proletarian) descent and is still preceded by a period of probation. Individuals are being chastised for "anti-Party activity," and weaknesses of the flesh are deemed "unworthy of a Party member." This language and ritual would make that nineteenth century rationalist Karl Marx cringe, and much of it would disgust Lenin himself. But the source of it all is in *What Is To Be Done?*

What is this collective hero to do? The Party is to fight "spontaneity" and "opportunism." Again the parallel with the medieval table of vices is irresistible. Spontaneity stands for our old friend: Sloth. In their historical march the working classes tend to acquiesce in petty material gains, lose all too easily their class and militant drive. The Party is to prod them, to explain their revolutionary tasks, and to endure until the victory is won. Opportunism is closely related to greed. How easy it is for the Socialist leaders to acquiesce in small victories and in concessions by the *bourgeoisie*, and to become tempted by parliamentary and ministerial positions, pushing the idea of a decisive assault upon capitalism farther and farther away from their minds. Again the Party knows how to accept, but never to rest content with concessions, just as it is capable of suffering a temporary defeat and then regrouping for a renewed assault. The Socialist (the temptation is great to write here anachronistically Bolshevik or Communist) should know how to avoid self-indulgence. And in the latter is found the source of terrorism. Overwrought intellectuals are incapable of patient and long-range revolutionary action. It is easier to commit an individual act of violence, but does not the whole history of the revolutionary movement show the futility of such acts?

The last point recalls us to a constant characteristic of Lenin's designs. No sooner is one tempted to feel condescending toward the theological, or, depending on taste, adolescent quality of his thinking, than one is sobered by his immense practicality and common sense. How childish and unrealistic at first glance is this concept of a Socialist Party as a body of revolutionary palladins, directed by the true faith of Marxism, unswerving in their devotion and uncorruptible. But, on the other hand, granted the premises of revolutionary socialism, what other model of a party can one construct for Russia in 1902? The weaknesses of his opponents' position are dissected most convincingly. The Socialist Revolutionaries and their penchant for terror have already been dealt with. The Economists talk and write as if Russia were a Western European state which grudgingly allows economic struggle by the workers. But in fact the Tsarist government will not allow free trade-union activity. The only unions it tolerates are those controlled by the police agents. There are those who complain about *Iskra's* (i.e., Lenin's) dictatorial and centralistic tendencies. But again Russia is not the West. You cannot have Kiev Socialists deliberating whether they will agree with their Odessa comrades or not. You dare not have each national group in the Empire have its own independent Socialist organization, the Jewish, Armenian, and other workers all pulling in different directions. There must be one centrally controlled Socialist Party speaking with one voice, composed not of well-intentioned people interested in political freedom and related ideas, but of active, professional revolutionaries.

What Is To Be Done? is not written in exaltation. It is not a messianic vision of a better world. On its face it is a laboriously, awkwardly written polemical pamphlet. Its flashes of insight, its hints of inspired revolutionary audacity are all but lost within the context of pedantic, organizational strictures and attacks upon groups and personalities, now only of historical interest. The ostensible targets of the tract, the Economists and their journal, *Rabocheye Delo* (*The Workers' Cause*), have long reposed, to use Trotsky's famous phrase, on "the rubbish heap of history." The people against whom Lenin exerted his fine Marxian vituperation, Krichevski, Struve, Bulgakov, Martynov, are now familiar only to the specialist in the period. Certainly to a contemporary Socialist they loomed as important as Lenin. Had Russia followed a constitutional and parliamentary path, as she seemed to promise between 1906 and 1914, it is their names which would enjoy the place of honor and importance in her history, while that of Vladimir Ulyanov-Lenin would now be known only to a historian. Though he could hardly have realized it, Lenin was writing a primer of politics for the twentieth century, a model for the movements—not only the Marxist ones—that have increasingly displaced liberalism and democracy.

Nikolai Valentinov

THE JACOBIN

Valentinov spent years in Siberian exile and tsarist prisons, sharing a fate common to most Russian revolutionaries of the 1890's. Escaping to Switzerland in 1904 he met Lenin in Geneva. At that time, Lenin, frustrated by Menshevik resistance to his egocentric and elitist conceptions of party organization, was beginning to think of removing his Bolshevik faction from the Russian Social Democratic party and establishing it as a separate party along Jacobin lines. Valentinov provides a fascinating portrait of Lenin's manic-depressive personality.

AT the end of January or the beginning of February [1904] Lenin began to write *One Step Forward, Two Steps Back*. During the three months which he took to write this book he underwent a startling change. Lenin, who was so strongly built, so full of vigour and vitality, became thin, with yellow sunken cheeks. His eyes, which were usually so lively, sly, and mocking, became dull and at times even quite dead. By the end of April, a glance was sufficient to show that either Lenin was ill or that he was fretting terribly over something.

* * *

This period now seems to me to have been one of the most important moments in Lenin's political life. He was at a turning-point. The choice before him was: should he go the way indicated by his dominating character, his whole cast of mind, his convictions and his ideology —that is to say, the way of the fully-fledged Bolshevism which eventually brought him to power in 1917? Or was he to take another road, to place various limits on himself, in the name of party unity, and make some concessions to the Mensheviks, all of which would be inconsistent with his belief in himself, his unshakable conviction that only he could organize a real revolutionary party and

lead it to great victories? Between February and the middle of April I frequently saw Lenin and went walking with him. He talked about what he was writing and what he would have liked to write. . . .

Lenin told me that at one of the Menshevik meetings some orator or other had tried to show that Lenin needed "a conductor's baton" in order to introduce discipline in the party "comparable to that which prevails in the barracks of . . . His Majesty's Guards."

"There you are," said Lenin, "that's the level of this debate. . . . They can't bring themselves to admit even now that if the party is to be led properly, and its members given jobs in accordance with their capacities and qualities, one has to put aside petty, cliquish considerations—and not worry about hurting people's feelings. The conductor's baton, even in an orchestra, is not given to the first person who comes along and asks for it or who happens to be able to read music. Even the drummer has to be able to read music. The right to wield the conductor's baton is given only to someone who has special qualities—first and foremost, the ability to organize. . . ."

It became quite obvious from what Lenin was saying that the right to the conductor's baton inside the party could belong only to him. Was this bombast, an

From Nikolay Valentinov, *Encounters with Lenin*, published by Oxford University Press, London, 1968, pp. 111–115, 127–128, 130–131, 146–151.

exaggerated vainglorious emphasis on his own special qualities and merits? No, his right was asserted with such simplicity and such certainty that he might have been saying: two and two make four. For Lenin this was simply a matter which required no proof. I was at first shocked by his unshakable faith in himself, which many years later I called his faith in his destiny, in his conviction that he was pre-ordained to carry out some great historical mission. In the following weeks little was left of my initial feeling, and this was not surprising—I found myself in Geneva in Lenin's entourage, in which no one for a moment doubted his right to hold the conductor's baton and to issue orders. Adherence to Bolshevism seemed somehow to imply a kind of oath of loyalty to Lenin, a vow to follow his lead unquestioningly. Since at that time there were no programmatic or tactical disagreements, conflict was reduced to differences in ideas on the structure of the party and the way it should be led, and this in the end always necessarily and inevitably came down to the role which Lenin wanted to play in the party and which his opponents refused to let him play. Whether those who took part in these debates wished it or not, every argument on party matters began and ended with the question of Lenin. Lenin did not go to these meetings and yet, though physically absent, he was there in spirit at all of them. No one seriously discussed any other Bolsheviks at all. The Geneva Mensheviks looked on the Bolsheviks as a claque, a set of puppets or a crowd of extras who were there only to carry out whatever Lenin had decided. Would there have been a split at the Congress, would the subsequent party dispute have arisen, if it had not been for Lenin? This question can with almost complete confidence be answered in the negative.

The Mensheviks began to feel that the constant preoccupation with Lenin's personality during the four months of post-Congress polemics, with its concomitant breaking off of all personal relations between many party workers, was an undesirable and dangerous thing. First, because this obsession with Lenin gave him more "specific gravity," greater importance than the Mensheviks would have wished to assign to him. Secondly, because the constant reiteration that Lenin was a bully, . . . that he was conceited, intolerant, power-loving, rude, quarrelsome and tactless, threatened to reduce the inner-party struggle to a clash of personalities—this would have played into Lenin's hands, since what he was trying to prove was that there were no differences of principle whatsoever, only the resentment and the hurt pride of the party "generals."

*   *   *

"Being a Marxist [Lenin once told me] does not mean learning Marxist formulae by heart. A parrot can do that. Marxism without appropriate deeds is nothing—only words, words, and more words. But for deeds, the right mentality is needed. The words of the [Mensheviks] are Marxist in outward appearance, but they have the mentality of wishy-washy intellectuals, individualists who have rebelled against proletarian discipline, against clear organizational forms, against firm party rules, against centralism, against everything that they can regard as a restriction on their 'psyche.' Their mentality is that of bourgeois democrats, not of socialists. . . . The bourgeois spinelessness of the [Mensheviks] and the whole incompatibility of their outlook with what revolutionary Marxism demands are best shown by their cries about 'conspiracy,' 'Blanquism,' 'Jacobinism.' How does Trotsky try to run me down? By calling me a Jacobin, a Robespierre. What does Akselrod try to frighten us with? With the warning that our movement might fall under the influence of a 'Jacobin club.' What did Martov say about the Jacobins at a meeting of the Mensheviks recently? That there could not be anything in common between Social Democracy and Jacobinism. . . . This panic fear of Jacobinism is common to all the Akimovs, Jaurèsists, Girondins, opportunists, and revisionists in Social Democracy today. The only difference is that in some cases it shows above the surface, while in others it remains hidden."

"I think," I said, "that we should, all the same, define what we mean by Jacobinism."

"There's no need to take that trouble. . . . Take the history of the French Revolution and you'll see what Jacobinism is. It is a struggle to achieve the end in view, with no shying away from drastic plebeian measures, a struggle without kid gloves, without tenderness, without fear of resorting to the guillotine. People like Bernstein[1] and Co., who think that democratic principles have absolute value cannot be Jacobins, of course. Rejection of the Jacobin method of struggle leads quite logically to rejection of the dictatorship of the proletariat, that is, of the coercion which is necessary and obligatory, which is indispensable for the smashing and annihilation of the enemies of the proletariat and for securing the victory of the socialist revolution. A proper bourgeois revolution cannot be carried out without a Jacobin purge—to say nothing of a socialist revolution. It requires a dictatorship, and the dictatorship of the proletariat requires a Jacobin mentality in the people who set it up. Everything is interconnected here. The dictatorship of the proletariat is an absolutely meaningless expression without Jacobin coercion."

*   *   *

"A revolutionary Social Democrat must be, cannot but be a Jacobin. You ask me what Jacobinism means. First of all, the Jacobinism of today demands recognition of the need for the dictatorship of the proletariat, since the victory of the proletariat cannot be consolidated without it. Secondly, Jacobinism calls for a centralized Party structure in order that this dictatorship be brought about. Rejection of this truth leads to organizational opportunism, which, in its turn, leads steadily, little by little, to the rejection of the dictatorship of the proletariat:

[1] German Marxist, founder of "revisionism." [Editor's note.]

all opponents of orthodox Marxism see eye to eye on this. Thirdly, Jacobinism demands real, strong discipline in the party in order to further the struggle. The outcries of the [Mensheviks] about 'blind subordination' and 'barrack discipline' reveal their love of anarchistic phrases, their slackness—typical of intellectuals—and their view of themselves as chosen spirits who stand outside and above the party laws drawn up by the party congress. If you take away discipline and frustrate centralism, where will the dictatorship find its support then? Dictatorship, centralism, strict and strong discipline—all these are connected logically, each complements the other. All this taken together is the Jacobinism which is being fought against, with Akselrod's blessing, by Martov, Akimov, and all the other Girondins. A revolutionary Social Democrat—this has to be grasped once and for all—must be and cannot but be a Jacobin. . . ."

"The Party's disease is now firmly diagnosed," he went on. "It is not just a matter of a few muddle-headed, hysterical people and windbags in the Party, what we have is a definitely revisionist right wing which is consciously disrupting and paralysing all party work under the guise of a struggle against 'Bonapartism.' . . . Things can't go on like this. Enough of this shilly-shallying. It is essential to . . . make it plain, in no uncertain terms, that we cannot stay in the same Party with these gentlemen any longer. They are our enemies, not our comrades. We must immediately establish our own press organ, otherwise we're finished. All representatives of the [Mensheviks] must be kicked out from the committees of the [Bolsheviks]; where this is not possible, parallel local committees must be formed which will consist exclusively of our people. As soon as possible we must call a congress of the representatives of the [Bolsheviks], which will announce the formation of an unswervingly revolutionary Marxist party, break off all contacts with the [Mensheviks] and openly proclaim the split that has once and for all taken place."

Lenin was an impetuous, passionate, and prejudiced man. His talk during our walks—about the Bund, Akimov, Aksel-rod, and Martov,[2] about the struggle at the Congress where, in his own words, he had "furiously slammed the door"—consisted of vicious and abusive invective. When he talked about the Mensheviks he could hardly control himself. He would suddenly stop in the middle of the pavement, stick his fingers into the holes of his waistcoat (even when he was wearing an overcoat), lean back, then jump forward, letting fly at his enemies. He cared nothing for the fact that passers-by stared with some amazement at his gesticulations. These tirades of his, which were delivered with such passion over a number of days, must undoubtedly have worn him out and used up some of his reserves of energy. After his attacks of rage, he became listless and gave way to hesitation and doubts. I draw attention to this for the following reasons. To my knowledge, Lenin's custom was to start writing early in the morning and keep on until lunch-time. After lunch he again sat down to write until 4 o'clock, when he went for a walk. However, although he went out for his walks in order to rest, the work on his book was not actually interrupted (he merely talked out loud instead of "whispering"), and he did not stop expending nervous energy. When he got back home, he resumed his writing, sometimes continuing until very late. . . .

I cannot end this chapter of my reminiscences without going a little farther into Lenin's peculiar psychological state which struck me so forcibly during my walks with him when he was writing the *Steps*. His frenzied state of "rage" and extreme nervous tension would be followed by exhaustion, decline of energy, listlessness, and depression. What I managed to find out about Lenin later, after his death, confirms beyond doubt that these alternating states were characteristic of his psychological make-up.

In his "normal" condition, Lenin tended towards an orderly life, free from all excesses. He wanted it to be regular, with precisely fixed hours for meals,

sleep, work, and leisure. He did not smoke or drink, and looked after his health, doing physical exercises every day. He was order and neatness incarnate. Every morning, before he settled down to read the newspapers, write, and work, Lenin, duster in hand, would put his desk and his books in order. He sewed any loose buttons on his coat or trousers himself, without bothering Krupskaya.[3] If he found a stain on his suit, he immediately tried to remove it with petrol. He kept his bicycle as clean as a surgical instrument. In this "normal" condition Lenin would have appeared to any observer as the most sober, balanced, and well-disciplined of men, without passions, repelled by slovenliness, and in particular by Bohemian ways. In such moments he liked to lead a quiet life reminiscent of his Simbirsk days. "I have already got used to the way of life in Cracow: it is limited, quiet, and sleepy," he wrote to his relatives in 1913. "No matter how god-forsaken this town may be, I like it better here than in Paris."

This equilibrium, this "normal" condition, occurred only from time to time, and was sometimes only of very short duration. Lenin was always breaking out of it, throwing himself into enthusiasms which gripped him completely. These enthusiasms were of a very special sort. There was always an element in them of frenzy, loss of proportion, and recklessness. Krupskaya, very aptly, called this *rage* (using the French form of the word). Various forms of Lenin's *rage* could easily be observed during his Siberian exile. Once, having bought a pair of skates in Minusinsk, he went skating both in the morning and in the afternoon; he startled the inhabitants of the village of Shushenskoye "with his gigantic steps and Spanish leaps," as Krupskaya puts it. "He liked to challenge us," writes Lepeshinsky. "Who will race me?" Ilyich would dart off ahead of everyone, exerting all his will-power and straining his muscles to the utmost to win at any price, whatever effort it cost him." Shooting was his second *rage*. Lenin provided himself with a gun and a dog and

---

[2] Opponents within the Russian Marxist movement. [Editor's note.]

[3] Lenin's wife. [Editor's note.]

scoured the forests, fields, and ravines searching for game till he was exhausted. He devoted himself to shooting with such "fervent passion," wrote Lepeshinsky, that he could cover "forty versts" a day "among the hummocks and marshes" in his hunt for game. Chess was his third *rage*. He could play chess from early morning till late at night, and the game obsessed him to such an extent that he used to rave about it in his sleep. . . . Krupskaya once heard him calling out, in a dream: "If he moves his knight here, I'll counter with my castle." There was also a fourth *rage*.

"Ilyich," Krupskaya wrote to her relatives, "used to say that he did not like mushrooms and would not pick them; but now you can't drag him out of the woods—he is in a real *rage* about mushrooms." He had several fits of this *rage*. In the summer of 1916 Lenin and Krupskaya were hurrying to catch their train, along the mountain paths that led from the holiday home at Schaudivisé, near Zürich. It started drizzling, and soon the drizzle turned into a downpour. Lenin noticed some white mushrooms in the woods, grew excited at once, and began to pick them, regardless of the rain. "We got soaked to the skin, and missed the train, of course": all the same, Lenin completely satisfied his *rage* for mushrooms; he stopped gathering them only after he had filled a whole bag.

He put this kind of *rage*—but with even greater fury—into his public, revolutionary, and intellectual activity. He wrote to Inessa Armand in 1916:

"That is my life! One fighting campaign after another. . . . It has been going on since 1893. And so has the hatred of the philistines on account of it! But still, I would not exchange this life for 'peace' with the philistines."

A fighting campaign! It cannot be put any better. Campaign against the Populists, campaign for the organization of the party and for the establishment of centralism and iron discipline in it, campaign for the boycott of the State Duma and for the armed uprising, campaign against the Menshevik "liquidators," campaign for the ideological annihilation of everyone who did not believe in dialectical materialism, campaign for the defeat of Russia in the war of 1914–17, campaign for the overthrow of the Provisional Government, for the seizure of power in order "either to perish or rush full steam ahead." Lenin's life was indeed spent in a succession of fighting campaigns, for which he mobilized all his intellectual and physical strength.

If his condition during his work on *One Step Forward* is any guide, I can well imagine what Lenin must have been like during all these "campaigns." Like an engine once it has been started, Lenin generated an incredible amount of energy in order to achieve his idea, his wish, his aim in whatever campaign he was engaged in, and make the members of his party obey him unconditionally. He did this in the steadfast belief that only he had the right to wield the "conductor's baton." Lenin became "rabid" during his attacks, as he himself admitted. The idea which had taken hold of him at any given moment totally dominated his mind, turning him into a man possessed. It seemed as if all other aspects of his mental life, all his other interests and wishes, were swept aside and vanished during such periods. There was one idea alone, nothing else, in Lenin's field of vision: one brightly shining point in the darkness, and in front of it a closed door upon which Lenin hammered violently, frenziedly, in order either to open it or to break it down. The enemy in the particular campaign might be Mikhaylovsky, the leader of the Populists, or the Menshevik Akselrod, or his party comrade Bogdanov, or Avenarius, the Zürich philosopher who had died long before and who had not been involved in politics in any way whatsoever. He violently hated all of them, wanted to "smash their faces in," to stick the convict's badge on them, to insult them, to trample them underfoot, to spit on them. He carried out the October Revolution too in a *rage* like this; and in order to win over his vacillating party to the idea of seizing power he did not shrink from calling some of its top leaders cowards, traitors, and idiots.

The tremendous expenditure of energy demanded by every campaign that Lenin undertook, driving himself and relentlessly urging others onward, wore him out and drained his strength. The engine of his will refused to work beyond a certain stage of frenzied tension. There was no more fuel for it left in his organism. Following an attack, or a series of attacks, of his *rage,* his energy would begin to ebb, and a psychological reaction set in: dullness, loss of strength, and fatigue which laid him out. He could neither eat nor sleep. Headaches tormented him. His face became sallow, even dark at times, the light died in his small, sharp Mongol eyes. I once saw him when he was in such a state. He was unrecognizable. To escape from his terrible depression, Lenin used to run away to rest in some quiet, solitary spot to put out of his head, at least for the time being, those thoughts which were lodged in it like a splinter; not to have to think about anything, and what was most important—not to have to see anyone, not to have to talk to anyone. Thus, after finishing *One Step Forward,* Lenin and Krupskaya went rambling in the mountains for several weeks. "We chose," Krupskaya remembered, "the loneliest paths, went to the remotest spots, so as to be as far as possible from people." We find Lenin in a similar condition in June 1907. The *rage* with which Lenin abused the liberal Cadets, called for armed uprising, and fought the Mensheviks, had sapped his strength to such an extent that he was half-dead when he returned to Kuokkala, in Finland, after the London congress of the party. Krupskaya immediately took him away so that he would be as far from people as possible, to Knipovich's country cottage at Stiersudden (Styrsudd), a very quiet little place in the heart of Finland. He could hardly walk, had no desire to talk, and spent almost the whole day with his eyes closed. He kept dropping off to sleep all the time. When he got to the woods "he would sit down under a fir-tree and fall asleep at once." The children from the neighbouring country cottage called him "sleepy-head." What Lenin wrote to his mother from Stiersudden when he began to come to life is very characteristic:

"The rest I am getting here is marvellous . . . no people, nothing to do. No people and nothing to do is the best thing for me."

This was Lenin with his guard down. He again completely lost his strength in Paris in 1909, after another party squabble and an exhausting campaign against Bogdanov, the Empiriocriticists, the "Otzovists," the "Vperyodists," and so forth. He escaped to the little village of Bombon in the *département* of Seine-et-Marne, he did not want to see or hear anyone, and only after three weeks of this "pastoral" life was he able to overcome the depression which had him in its grip. He was again shattered when he returned from the 1915 Zimmerwald Conference, where he had fought frantically for a policy of transforming the imperialist war into a civil war. He sought rest at Sörenberg, a little spot near Berne, at the foot of the Rothorn. On his arrival he climbed the mountain and then "suddenly lay down on the ground" where he stood, or, to be more exact, dropped like someone who had been shot, "very awkwardly, almost onto the snow, and then passed out and slept like a log." Krupskaya, who was already familiar with this alternation of the highest flights with the deepest mental and physical exhaustion, wrote sadly: "It was clear that the Zimmerwald Conference had worn his nerves out and used up practically all his strength."

Lenin wrote to Gorky on 9 July 1921: "I am so tired, I can do *nothing at all.*" It would be worth following into the period after October 1917 the ebbs and flows of Lenin's *rage,* which eventually turned this impetuous man into a paralytic incapable of speaking or of moving his arms and legs. But this would go far beyond the limits of these notes of mine.

That was what Lenin was like. The condition of his mind cannot possibly be represented "graphically" by an even line. His mental graph was a line which soared up only to plummet to the lowest possible point. It would seem that people like this, subject to such jumps in their cerebral system, are bound to die of haemorrhage of the brain, as Lenin did . . . .

Bertram D. Wolfe

CREATOR OF TOTALITARIANISM

Bertram D. Wolfe was initially sympathetic to Lenin's revolution and managed to make the personal acquaintance of many of its leaders, including Stalin, Trotsky, Bukharin and Molotov. In time he soured and became hostile to all that the Soviet Union stood for. His *Three Who Made a Revolution,* published in 1948, was widely hailed for its perceptive comment on the origins of Bolshevism's big three. Since then he has published extensively on numerous aspects of the communist movement, has taught at many leading universities—Oxford, Geneva, and the University of California among them—and was eventually appointed to his present post as Senior Research Associate at the Hoover Institution for the Study of War, Revolution and Peace.

IN LENIN, Marx had an innovating disciple who was a theoretician, a technician, a militant defender, propounder, and virtuoso of organization and total power. Conspirative secrecy, centralized organization, command performance, military discipline, detailed instructions, the ability to mobilize, manipulate, and organize discontent and hatred—a technique, indeed an elaborate technology and pedantic systemization of the art and science of seizing power, extending power by frontal attack or by zigzag and by feeling out the weak spots in the adversary, a technique and technology for holding power, utilizing power, regularizing and bureaucratizing power, extending power in width and depth even unto the affairs of the spirit—what are these if not the levers of modern totalitarian revolution and totalitarian rule?

The first peculiarity that strikes one in Lenin's organizational doctrine is his centralism, and his extreme distrust not only of whole classes (the intelligentsia, the petty bourgeoisie, the peasantry, and the working class itself), but even of the rank and file of his own Party, and his own local organizations. In 1904 he wrote:

Bureaucratism *versus* autonomy, such is the principle of revolutionary social democracy as against the opportunists. The organization of revolutionary social democracy strives to go from the top downward, and defends the enlargement of the rights and plenary powers of the Central Body.

In the third year of his rule, with his power secure and the civil war at an end, far from permitting the principle of centralism to "erode," he reinforced it by plugging the last vents of public discussion with cement. It was then that he abolished the very basis of such party democracy as had existed in the early years before he could complete the act of *Gleichschaltung** by prohibiting party groupings, platforms for proposal of changes, gatherings of like-minded communists to discuss their views, with expulsion provided for any violation. Having already drained the Constituent Assembly and the Soviets of political power, he now did the same with the trade unions and his own party.

In power Lenin was fulfilling the dream of his early "Letter to a Comrade

* A word used in Hitler's Germany to signify that the entire situation was moving in time to the same beat. [Editor's note.]

From Bertram D. Wolfe, "Reflections on the Future of the Soviet System," *The Russian Review,* April 1967, pp. 113–116, 123–126.

on Our Organizational Tasks" which had so impressed Stalin:

We have arrived at an extremely important principle of all party organization and activity. In regard to ideological and practical *direction,* the movement and the revolutionary struggle of the proletariat need the *greatest* possible *centralization,* but in regard to *keeping the center informed* . . . in regard to *responsibility* before the party, we need the greatest possible *decentralization.* The movement must be led by the smallest possible number. . . . But the largest possible number of the most varied and heterogeneous groups drawn from diverse layers of the proletariat (and other classes) should take part in the movement. . . . *Now* we become an organized party and that means the creation of power, the transformation of the authority of ideas into the authority of power, the subordination of the lower party organs to the higher ones.

Here, as early as 1902, is Lenin's whole schema: the dictatorship of the party over all classes of society, the transmission belt system of implementing that dictatorship, the rule of the many and most diverse groups by the fewest and most homogeneous, the transformation of the authority of ideas into the authority of power in all the manifold activities which were to concern the party—and which activities were not?

Lenin's Archimedean cry for an organization of revolutionaries to turn Russia upsidedown did not cease when he had indeed turned Russia upsidedown. As before he continued to call for "organization, organization, organization." To his old dream of centralized organization of the party, he added the new dream made possible by power: the dream of total organization of life by the party in accordance with its, *i.e.,* his blueprint for society and man.

Now he would remake the spirit of Russia, its industries, its agriculture, its interchange of goods, its foreign trade. He would remake the Oblomovs, the Lopakhins, the Ranevskayas, the Stroganovs, the Morozovs, and even the Ivan Ivanoviches, all according to his blueprint of the New Soviet Man. He would remake Russia's emotions, her thoughts, her feelings, her habits, even her dreams, eliminating by total organization all slackness, all waywardness of will, all indifference to or tolerance of other ways. "We must organize everything," he said in the summer of 1918, "take everything into our hands." To the authoritarianism inherent in an infallible doctrine, possessed and interpreted by an infallible interpreter who rules an infallible party infallibly from above, Lenin added the further dream of "organizing everything, taking everything in our hands."

Thus the most obvious trait setting Lenin apart from his associates in the Russian intelligentsia and the revolutionary movement was his absorption with the mechanics and dynamics of organization and power. In a world where most intellectuals were in love with ideas, and accustomed—whether by temperament or the pressure of circumstances—to a distinction, even a yearning gap, between the dream and the deed, Lenin was an organization man—indeed, the organization man of whatever movements he took part in. When he broke with his colleagues on *Iskra* it was on the question of organization. Amidst men dedicated to dreams, organization was his dream. But such an ideology, the ideology of complete control of society by the party, and complete centralization of power within the party, does not erode as easily as do other ideas such as egalitarianism, or international socialism, or permanent revolution or "complete communism."

In other words, totalitarianism has an ideology that is the ideology of a structure. What is growing thin, shallow, passionless, and lacking in conviction is the ideology of the structure's purpose. Every effort is made to diminish or check this process of "erosion" by the enforcement of *partiinost,* by the exclusion of the foreign press, radio and television, by the deliberate suppression of articles of criticism or challenge, by a continuing war on freedom in the arts, and where they impinge on matters of power, in the sciences, by the outlandish denunciation of "archive rats" (Stalin), "historians" (they are "dangerous people"—Khrushchev), "bourgeois objectivity," "bourgeois falsification," and "vulgar factology." . . .

Fifty years have passed since Lenin seized power and established his dictatorship which has proved by a half century of continuity and contained change to be the most durable institutional regime, or, if you wish the most durable "party" regime, in the modern world. Yet one of its striking peculiarities is that in the course of a half century it has not succeeded in establishing a legitimate mode of succession. . . .

Once Lenin had power in his hands and those of his Party, he laid his plans to prevent the establishment of a new democratic legitimacy: "We say to the people that their interests are higher than the interests of a democratic institution. It is not necessary to go back to the old prejudices which subordinate the interests of the people to formal democracy."

With the forestalling of the constituent assembly by his seizure of power, and the rupture of democratic legitimacy by the dispersal by force of the only authorized representatives of the Russian people, Lenin bade farewell to legitimacy and established a permanent dictatorship.

There no longer was hereditary monarchical legitimacy or democratic legitimacy or any thought of prelegitimacy. In a half-century the dictatorial regime has not once submitted its actions or its personnel to the approval of the Soviet people in a free election, nor can it, nor has it the intention to do so in the future.

What then was the basis of Lenin's claim to rule over a great nation? Simply this: We have made a revolution in one nation with the intent to use it as a springboard for world revolution. We Communists have seized power over this nation because we possess an infallible doctrine that lets us know what history wants our country to do and to be. We are the sole possessors and only true interpreters of a "scientific" and infallible doctrine that enables us to work out a blueprint for the remaking of the Soviet Union and the remaking of man. It is this which justifies the dictatorship

that we have set up over our own people, and aim to extend to all the lands on earth.

Lenin said on December 5, 1919, after he had been exercising power for two years, "Dictatorship is a harsh, heavy and even bloody word." And a year later, on October 20, 1920, he explained with precise pedantry to doubting democrats:

The scientific concept *dictatorship* means nothing more nor less than unrestricted power, not limited by anything, not restrained by any laws, nor by any absolute rules, and resting directly on force, *that, and nothing else but that,* is the meaning of the concept, dictatorship.

In short, all limitations, constitutional, traditional, legal, or moral, were ruptured. Having taken power by force in the name of their blueprint, the dictators were to apply their blueprint without accepting any restraint upon their use of force. For such a regime, though it last a half-century, no legitimacy is sought nor possible.

Instead, there were four pieces of semantic sleight-of-hand employed by Lenin, but these were only meant to paralyze the enemy and lessen opposition.

The first is the confusing of the proletariat with the people. The second is the confusing of the Party with the proletariat. The third is the confusing of the Party Machine with the Party. The fourth is the confusing of the *Vozhd* or Leader or Boss with the Party Machine. All four of these semantic tricks are inventions of Lenin. As hypocrisy is said to be the tribute that vice pays to virtue, so these subterfuges are the tribute that dictatorship pays to democracy. They have grown stale by endless repetition but Lenin's heirs . . . do not dare dispense with them lest their world come tumbling down.

As we probe the fictions, they dissolve before our eyes. The party is no party, for a party means a part and where there are no contending parties, life dies out in the single party.

From her prison cell Rosa Luxemburg admonished Lenin: "Freedom for the supporters of the government alone, freedom only for the members of one party—that is no freedom at all. . . . All that is instructive, wholesome, and purifying in political freedom depends upon this essential characteristic. . . . With the repression of political life in the land as a whole, life in the Soviets must also become more and more crippled. Without general elections, without unrestricted freedom of press and assembly, without a free struggle of opinion, life will die out in every public institution. . . . Public life gradually falls asleep, a few dozen leaders . . . direct and rule. . . . An elite of the working class is invited from time to time to meetings where they are to applaud the speeches of the leaders and approve resolutions unanimously. [It is] not the dictatorship of the proletariat but of a handful of politicians, a clique. . . . Such conditions must inevitably cause a brutalization of public life: attempted assassinations, shooting of hostages, etc."

How grimly has history confirmed her prophetic vision! What she did not foresee, however, was that Lenin himself would finally drain his own party of all political life by prohibiting groupings, and that his successor would kill more members of his own party than all the enemies of communism in the world put together.

Maxim Gorky

NAPOLEON OF SOCIALISM

In the decade before 1917 Maxim Gorky, titan of Russian letters and an avowed foe of tsarism, had frequently debated with his close friend, Lenin. The God-seeking Gorky was usually trying to instill some simple human feelings into the heart of the cold-blooded revolutionary warrior whom he so admired. But his efforts met with no success: After 1917, Gorky, horrified by the excesses of the Bolshevik dictatorship, used his newspaper *Novaya Zhizn* (New Life) to express his anger toward his former brother-in-arms.

TO THE DEMOCRACY

Novaya Zhizn, No. 174, November 7 (20) 1917

THE socialist ministers released by Lenin and Trotsky from the Peter and Paul Fortress went home, leaving their colleagues M. V. Bernatsky, A. I. Konovalov, M. I. Tereshchenko, and others in the hands of people who have no conception of the freedom of the individual or of the rights of man.

Lenin, Trotsky, and their companions have already become poisoned with the filthy venom of power, and this is evidenced by their shameful attitude toward freedom of speech, the individual, and the sum total of those rights for the triumph of which democracy struggled.

Blind fanatics and dishonest adventurers are rushing madly, supposedly along the road to the "social revolution"; in reality this is the road to anarchy, to the destruction of the proletariat and of the revolution.

On this road Lenin and his associates consider it possible to commit all kinds of crimes, such as the slaughter outside St. Petersburg, the destruction of Moscow, the abolition of freedom of speech, and senseless arrests—all the abomina-tions which Pleve and Stolypin[1] once perpetrated.

Of course, Stolypin and Pleve went against democracy, against all that was live and decent in Russia. Lenin, how-ever, is followed by a rather sizeable— for the time being—portion of the work-ers; but I believe that the good sense of the working class and its awareness of its historical tasks will soon open the eyes of the proletariat to the utter im-possibility of realizing Lenin's promises, to all the depth of his madness, and to his Nechaev[2] and Bakunin brand of an-archism.

The working class cannot fail to under-stand that Lenin is only performing a certain experiment on their skin and on their blood, that he is striving to push the revolutionary mood of the proletariat to its furthest extreme and see—what will come of this?

Of course, he does not believe in the possibility of the victory of the proletariat

[1] Pleve and Stolypin were leading ministers in the government of Nicholas II. Pleve was as-sassinated in 1904; Stolypin, in 1911. [Editor's note.]

[2] Nechaev was a fanatical conspirator of the 1860s who became famous for creating a revo-lutionary morality that turned the revolution-ary into a depersonalized engine of destruction. [Editor's note.]

Reprinted with the permission of the publisher from Maxim Gorky, *Untimely Thoughts, Essays, on Revolution, Culture and the Bolsheviks, 1917–1918* (New York: Paul S. Eriksson, 1968), pp. 85–89.

in Russia under the present conditions, but perhaps he is hoping for a miracle.

The working class should know that miracles do not occur in real life, that they are to expect hunger, complete disorder in industry, disruption of transportation, and protracted bloody anarchy followed by a no less bloody and gloomy reaction.

This is where the proletariat is being led by its present leader, and it must be understood that Lenin is not an omnipotent magician but a cold-blooded trickster who spares neither the honor nor the life of the proletariat.

The workers must not allow adventurers and madmen to heap shameful, senseless, and bloody crimes on the head of the proletariat, for which not Lenin but the proletariat itself will pay.

I ask:

Does the Russian democracy remember the ideas for the triumph of which it struggled against the despotism of the monarchy?

Does it consider itself capable of continuing this struggle now?

Does it remember that when the Romanov gendarmes threw its ideological leaders into prisons and hard-labor camps, it called this method of struggle base?

In what way does Lenin's attitude toward freedom of speech differ from the same attitude of a Stolypin, a Pleve, and other half-humans?

Does not Lenin's government, as the Romanov government did, seize and drag off to prison all those who think differently?

Why are Bernatsky, Konovalov, and other members of the coalition government sitting in the fortress? Are they in any way more criminal than their socialist colleagues freed by Lenin?

The only honest answer to these questions must be an immediate demand to free the ministers and other innocent people who were arrested, and also to restore freedom of speech in its entirety.

Then the sensible elements of the democracy must draw further conclusions, they must decide: is the road of conspirators and anarchists of Nechaev's type also their road?

FOR THE ATTENTION OF THE WORKERS

Novaya Zhizn, No. 177, November 10 (23), 1917

Vladimir Lenin is introducing a socialist order in Russia by Nechaev's method —"full steam ahead through the swamp."

Both Lenin and Trotsky and all the others who are accompanying them to their ruin in the quagmire of reality are evidently convinced, along with Nechaev, that "the easiest way to make a Russian follow you is to give him the right to act dishonorably," and so they cold-bloodedly dishonor the revolution and dishonor the working class by forcing it to organize bloody slaughter and by inciting it to outrages and the arresting of completely innocent people such as A. V. Kartashev, M. V. Bernatsky, A. I. Konovalov, and others.

Having forced the proletariat to agree to abolish freedom of the press, Lenin and his cronies thus gave the enemies of democracy the legitimate right to shut its mouth. Threatening with hunger and violence all who do not agree with the despotism of Lenin and Trotsky, these "leaders" justify the despotism of authority against which all the best forces of the country fought so painfully long.

"The obedience of schoolboys and fools" who together follow Lenin and Trotsky "has reached the highest point"; cursing their leaders behind their backs, now leaving them, now joining them again, the schoolboys and fools, in the end, humbly serve the will of the dogmatists and arouse more and more the unrealizable hope for a carefree life among the most unenlightened masses of soldiers and workers.

Imagining themselves to be Napoleons of socialism, the Leninists rant and rave, completing the destruction of Russia. The Russian people will pay for this with lakes of blood.

Lenin himself, of course, is a man of exceptional strength. For twenty-five years he stood in the front rank of those who fought for the triumph of socialism. He is one of the most prominent and striking figures of international social democracy; a man of talent, he possesses all the qualities of a "leader" and also the lack of morality necessary for this role, as well as an utterly pitiless attitude, worthy of a nobleman, toward the lives of the popular masses.

Lenin is a "leader" *and* a Russian nobleman, not without certain psychological traits of this extinct class, and therefore he considers himself justified in performing with the Russian people a cruel experiment which is doomed to failure beforehand.

The people, worn out and impoverished by war, have already paid for this experiment with thousands of lives and will be compelled to pay with tens of thousands, and this will deprive the nation of its leadership for a long time to come.

This inevitable tragedy does not disturb Lenin, the slave of dogma, or his cronies—his slaves. Life in all its complexity is unknown to Lenin, he does not know the popular masses, he has not lived with them; but he—from books—has learned how to raise these masses on their hind legs and how—easiest of all—to enrage their instincts. The working class is for a Lenin what ore is for a metalworker. Is it possible, under all present conditions, to mold a socialist state from this ore? Apparently it is impossible; however—why not try? What does Lenin risk if the experiment should fail?

He works like a chemist in a laboratory, with the difference that the chemist uses dead matter, but his work produces a valuable result for life; Lenin, however, works with living material and he is leading the revolution to ruin. Sensible workers who follow Lenin should realize that a pitiless experiment is being performed on the Russian working class, an experiment which will destroy the best forces of the workers and will arrest normal development of the Russian revolution for a long time to come.

Louis Fischer

CYNICAL AUTOCRAT

In nearly a half century as a roving reporter, beginning around 1920, Louis Fischer has written many books on the passing global and, particularly, the Soviet scene. He has spent over fourteen years in Russia, and his book *The Soviets in World Affairs* remains a classic account of the first decade of Soviet foreign policy. His biography of Lenin, written under the auspices of the Princeton Institute for Advanced Study, received the 1965 National Book Award for History and Biography.

NOBODY has recorded a Lenin laugh at himself for writing *The State and Revolution*. Perhaps he was too bitter to be amused.

After Lenin became master of the Soviet state, withering away did commence immediately, but what commenced to wither away was the idea of withering away. This manifested itself in big and little things. One such "minor" matter was revealed in 1960 in a Soviet magazine which published the reminiscences of P. Shumyakov, a Petrograd worker, about his encounters with Lenin in 1918. Starvation stalked the great city. The daily food ration consisted of 100 to 125 grams of bread doled out irregularly and an occasional head of a herring or a morsel of stale dried fish. Active communists with extra political assignments lacked the physical energy to cope with them. The communists of the Viborg district of Petrograd accordingly discussed the question of establishing a closed restaurant where party members might take more nourishing meals. Some communists, writes Shumyakov, thought that active party workers should starve just like the workingmen; "but the majority took a different view"—that if the communists were physically exhausted the result would be "inevitable premature collapse with disastrous effects on the revolution," because without its organizers and leaders "the working class would fail as the motor of the revolution and the builder of a new society." This problem was brought to Lenin.

Lenin listened to the opponents of privilege and rejected their arguments. He said, "The heroics of personal self-sacrifice, which is their basic position, are, especially in present conditions, profoundly petty bourgeois. . . . The working class cannot march in the vanguard of the revolution without its activists, its organizers. The activists have to be cared for, and at the present time, within the limits of existing possibilities, must be supported physically. A closed restaurant [Lenin declared] should be organized. The workers will understand the necessity of it." A few days later, Shumyakov recalls, the restaurant for the district (communist party) activists "was organized."

Shumyakov met Lenin again in Moscow in September, 1918. During the previous month a workers' squad in Petrograd had arrested two persons, " 'His Excellency,' the brother of 'His Excellency' Count Witte," a former tsarist prime minister, and, Shumyakov's memoir continues, "Voronin, the director-manager of 'The Voronin, Lyutch, and Chesser Stock Company.' " They were arrested and handed over to the Cheka for hoarding large quantities of canned goods, gold, bonds, and so forth. "Later we were informed that when the workers learned of the removal of the arrested men to the Cheka prison on Pea Street, they assembled and lynched them." Shumyakov reported this to Lenin. "Lenin," Shumyakov writes, "especially liked my story of the way we carried out the red terror in our district and in particular of the workers' violent reprisals against 'His Excellency Witte' and Manufacturer Voronin. In reply to my remark about our carelessness which resulted in the lynching, Vladimir Ilyich [Lenin] said, 'Well, there's no great harm in that, the workers knew whom they were punishing. In the course of a revolution such cases are undesirable but unavoidable.' "

Lenin's attitude to the closed restaurant for communists was sensible. His reaction to the lynching was practical; what's done is spilt milk even if it's blood. But privilege for communists and workers' license for red terror were the thin wedge of an ax that severed reality from the proclaimed ideal. Multiplied many times, applied to millions of communist and noncommunist servants of the state, the infringement of Lenin's rule that no official receive more than a workingman—today, the very notion would evoke horror and laughter in communist countries—has created a caste-conscious, status-seeking, luxury-lusting hierarchy who for decades have been sacrificing principle to power and justifying the most inhuman means by recourse to convenient, self-formulated ends that bear little resemblance to the goals born in the brains of Marx, Engels, and Lenin. In domestic policy and especially in international affairs the Soviet state accommodated itself to old Russia, to the sick psychology of Stalin, to necessity, and to opportunity. Lenin's *The State and Revolution* lies in the museum. The book is unique in all of Lenin's writings in that it is non-Marxist. For Lenin, the essence of Marxism was the class war. That, indeed, is the heart of Marx' and Lenin's teachings. But *The State and Revolution* shuts out the internal class war and the international class war. Adopting the utopian Nowhere (*Erewhon*) method he so reviled, Lenin described and prescribed a stateless society unrelated to reality then or in the foreseeable future or now in Russia and elsewhere. Despite its plethora of Marx-Engels terminology and quotations, the Lenin book is an aberrant intellectual enterprise, a fanciful exercise for so rock-hard a man, as un-Leninist as the mask he wore and the false name he bore in hiding while writing it.

Lenin admitted that the "*future* withering away" must "obviously be a rather lengthy process." But it would begin immediately after the overthrow of the bourgeoisie: "once the majority of the people *itself* suppresses its oppressors, a 'special force' for suppression is *no longer necessary*. In this sense the state *begins to wither away*."

Lenin was no sooner in government than the civil war and foreign intervention conduced to the aggrandizement of state power. Lenin also demonstrated, in deeds, from November, 1917, to his final illness that he believed in the greatest possible concentration of power in the single party that controlled the state. This was his prerevolutionary goal and his postrevolutionary practice. Party monocracy conformed with his principles and suited his willful personality. Autocracy also flowed from Russia's past. Lenin slipped back into it by subjective inclination and the force of objective circumstances. The root of the evil may lie in the fact that a minority and not the majority of the people suppressed their oppressors. Therefore "the special force," the state, prevailed.

Twenty months after his party seized the Russian state, Lenin went to Moscow's Sverdlov University and delivered a lecture—July 11, 1919—"On the State." Now the experienced statesman spoke. What had he learned? Lenin described the state, all states: "It has always been a definite kind of apparatus which differentiated itself from society and consisted of groups of persons who occupy themselves only, or almost only, or chiefly only with administration. People are divided between the administered and specialists who administer, who raise themselves above society and who are called the governors, the governors of the state. This apparatus, this group of people, which administers others, always takes over the apparatus of compulsion, physical force. . . ."

Still later Lenin came full circle and, dialectically negating the negation, he discarded his theory of the withering away of the state. It happened, fittingly, at a meeting on March 6, 1920, of the Moscow Soviet celebrating the first birthday of the Comintern. He told the assembled communists that it was "impossible to put the question of the state in the old way; in place of the old, bookish formulation of this question a new, practical formulation has appeared as a result of the revolutionary movement. . . . So now the question of the state has been set on different rails. . . . To object to the necessity of a central government, of a dictatorship, of the unity of will has become impossible."

The State and Revolution, mocked by the revolution, has been scrapped by its revolutionary author—a courageous act. Life killed a beautiful theory. Instead of the death of the state, the death of *The State and Revolution.*

V. I. Lenin

HERALD OF THE PROLETARIAN STATE

The following is from the lengthy article "Can the Bolsheviks Retain State Power?" written by Lenin October 7–14, 1917, that is, just weeks before the seizure of power by his party. In the article Lenin sought to prove that 240,000 Bolsheviks would be able to govern Russia since they would be "governing in the interests of the poor against the rich," and he asserted that the Soviets constituted a ready-made device to take over and run the state's machinery. The 240,000 Bolsheviks, moreover, represented a million, for, as the experience of Europe and Russia had established, the number of votes a party drew in an election was always about one-fourth of its actual following. "So here we have already a 'state apparatus' ... devoted to the socialist state ... out of idealism." Lenin justifies the revolutionary state's use of violence and terror against members of the former oppressive class; but his prior conceptions of the means that would be used to crush resistance turned out to be far milder than the brutal policies his regime actually put into practice.

I T is merely a question of breaking the resistance of an insignificant minority of the population, literally a handful of people, over each of whom the employees' unions, the trade unions, the consumers' societies and the Soviets will institute such *supervision* that every Tit Titych[1] will be *surrounded* as the French were at Sedan. We know these Tit Tityches by name: we only have to consult the lists of directors, board members, large shareholders, etc. There are several hundred, at most several thousand of them in the *whole* of Russia, and the proletarian state, with the apparatus of the Soviets, of the employees' unions, etc., will be able to appoint ten or even a hundred supervisors to each of them, so that instead of "breaking resistance" it may even be possible, by means of *workers' control* (over the capitalists), to make all resistance *impossible*.

The important thing will not be even the confiscation of the capitalists' property, but country-wide, all-embracing

workers' control over the capitalists and their possible supporters. Confiscation alone leads nowhere, as it does not contain the element of organisation, of accounting for proper distribution. ...

Two circumstances must be considered here to supplement what has already been said. In the first place, the new means of control have been created *not* by us, but by capitalism in its military-imperialist stage; and in the second place, it is important to introduce more democracy into the *administration* of a proletarian state.

The grain monopoly and bread rationing were introduced not by us, but by the capitalist state in war-time. It had already introduced universal labour conscription within the framework of capitalism, which is war-time penal servitude for the workers. But here too, as in all its history-making activities, the proletariat takes its weapons from capitalism and does not "invent" or "create them out of nothing."

The grain monopoly, bread rationing and labour conscription in the hands of the proletarian state, in the hands of

[1] A tyrannical merchant ridiculed in one of Russia's famous plays. [Editor's note.]

From V. I. Lenin, *Collected Works*, Vol. XXVI (Moscow: Progress Publishers, 1964), pp. 107–118.

sovereign Soviets, will be the most powerful means of accounting and control, means which, applied to the capitalists, and to *the rich in general,* applied to them by the *workers,* will provide a force unprecedented in history for "setting the state apparatus in motion," for overcoming the resistance of the capitalists, for subordinating them to the proletarian state. These means of control and of *compelling people to work* will be more potent than the laws of the Convention and its guillotine. The guillotine *only* terrorised, only broke *active* resistance. *For us, this is not enough.*

For us, this is not enough. We must not only "terrorise" the capitalists, i.e., make them feel the omnipotence of the proletarian state and give up all idea of actively resisting it. We must also break *passive* resistance, which is undoubtedly more dangerous and harmful. We must not only break resistance of every kind. We must also *compel the capitalists to work* within the framework of the new state organisation. It is not enough to "remove" the capitalists; we must (after removing the undesirable and incorrigible "resisters") employ them *in the service of the new state.* This applies both to the capitalists and to the upper section of the bourgeois intellectuals, office employees, etc.

And we have the means to do this. The means and instruments for this have been placed in our hands by the capitalist state in the war. These means are the grain monopoly, bread rationing and labour conscription. "He who does not work, neither shall he eat"—this is the fundamental, the first and most important rule the Soviets of Workers' Deputies can and will introduce when they become the ruling power.

Every worker has a work-book. This book does not degrade him, although *at present* it is undoubtedly a document of capitalist wage-slavery, certifying that the workman belongs to some parasite.

The Soviets will introduce work-books *for the rich* and *then* gradually for the whole population (in a peasant country work-books will probably not be needed for a long time for the overwhelming majority of the peasants). The work-book will cease to be the badge of the "common herd," a document of the "lower" orders, a certificate of wage-slavery. It will become a document certifying that in the new society there are no longer any "workmen," nor, on the other hand, are there any longer men *who do not work.*

The rich will be obliged to get a work-book from the workers' or office employees' union with which their occupation is most closely connected, and every week, or other definite fixed period, they will have to get from that union a certificate to the effect that they are performing their work conscientiously; without this they will not be able to receive bread ration cards or provisions in general. The proletarian state will say: we need good organisers of banking and the amalgamation of enterprises (in this matter the capitalists have more experience, and it is easier to work with experienced people), and we need far, far more engineers, agronomists, technicians and scientifically trained specialists of every kind than were needed before. We shall give all these specialists work to which they are accustomed and which they can cope with; in all probability we shall introduce complete wage equality only gradually and shall pay these specialists higher salaries during the transition period. We shall place them, however, under comprehensive workers' control and we shall achieve the complete and absolute operation of the rule "He who does not work, neither shall he eat." We shall not invent the organisational form of the work, but take ready-made from capitalism—we shall take over the banks, syndicates, the best factories, experimental stations, academies, and so forth; all that we shall have to do is to borrow the best models furnished by the advanced countries.

Of course, we shall not in the least descend to a utopia, we are not deserting the soil of most sober, practical reason when we say that the entire capitalist class will offer the most stubborn resistance, but this resistance will be broken by the organisation of the entire population in Soviets. Those capitalists who are exceptionally stubborn and recalcitrant will, of course, have to be punished by the confiscation of their whole property and by imprisonment. . . .

The proletariat, we are told, will not be able to set the state apparatus in motion.

Since the 1905 revolution, Russia has been governed by 130,000 landowners, who have perpetrated endless violence against 150,000,000 people, heaped unconstrained abuse upon them, and condemned the vast majority to inhuman toil and semi-starvation.

Yet we are told that the 240,000 members of the Bolshevik Party will not be able to govern Russia, govern her in the interests of the poor and against the rich. These 240,000 are already backed by no less than a million votes of the adult population, for this is precisely the proportion between the number of Party members and the number of votes cast for the Party that has been established by the experience of Europe and the experience of Russia as shown, for example, by the elections to the Petrograd City Council last August. We therefore already have a "state apparatus" of *one million* people devoted to the socialist state for the sake of high ideals and not for the sake of a fat sum received on the 20th of every month.

In addition to that we have a "magic way" to enlarge our state apparatus *tenfold* at once, at one stroke, a way which no capitalist state ever possessed or could possess. This magic way is to draw the working people, to draw the poor, into the daily work of state administration.

To explain how easy it will be to employ this magic way and how faultlessly it will operate, let us take the simplest and most striking example possible.

The state is to forcibly evict a certain family from a flat and move another in. This often happens in the capitalist state, and it will also happen in our proletarian or socialist state.

The capitalist state evicts a working-class family which has lost its breadwinner and cannot pay the rent. The bailiff appears with police, or militia, a whole squad of them. To effect an eviction in a working-class district a whole detachment of Cossacks is required. Why? Because the bailiff and the militiaman refuse to go without a very strong military guard. They know that the scene of an eviction arouses such fury among the neighbours, among thousands and thousands of people who have been driven to the verge of desperation, arouses such hatred towards the capitalists and the capitalist state, that the bailiff and the squad of militiamen run the risk of being torn to pieces at any minute. Large military forces are required, several regiments must be brought into a big city, and the troops must come from some distant, outlying region so that the soldiers will not be familiar with the life of the urban poor, so that the soldiers will not be "infected" with socialism.

The proletarian state has to forcibly move a very poor family into a rich man's flat. Let us suppose that our squad of workers' militia is fifteen strong; two sailors, two soldiers, two class-conscious workers (of whom, let us suppose, only one is a member of our Party, or a sympathiser), one intellectual, and eight from the poor working people, of whom at least five must be women, domestic servants, unskilled labourers, and so forth. The squad arrives at the rich man's flat, inspects it and finds that it consists of five rooms occupied by two men and two women—"You must squeeze up a bit into two rooms this winter, citizens, and prepare two rooms for two families now living in cellars. Until the time, with the aid of engineers (you are an engineer, aren't you?), we have built good dwellings for everybody, you will have to squeeze up a little. Your telephone will serve ten families. This will save a hundred hours of work wasted on shopping, and so forth. Now in your family there are two unemployed persons who can perform light work: a citizeness fifty-five years of age and a citizen fourteen years of age. They will be on duty for three hours a day supervising the proper distribution of provisions for ten families and keeping the necessary account of this. The student citizen in our squad will now write out this state order in two copies and you will be kind enough to give us a signed declaration that you will faithfully carry it out."

This, in my opinion, can illustrate how the distinction between the old bourgeois and the new socialist state apparatus and state administration could be illustrated.

We are not utopians. We know that an unskilled labourer or a cook cannot immediately get on with the job of state administration. In this we agree with the Cadets, with Breshkovskaya, and with Tsereteli.* We differ, however, from these citizens in that we demand an immediate break with the prejudiced view that only the rich, or officials chosen from rich families, are capable of *administering* the state, of performing the ordinary, everyday work of administration. We demand that *training* in the work of state administration be conducted by class-conscious workers and soldiers and that this training be begun at once, i.e., that a *beginning* be made at once in training all the working people, all the poor, for this work.

We know that the Cadets are also willing to teach the people democracy. Cadet ladies are willing to deliver lectures to domestic servants on equal rights for women in accordance with the best English and French sources. And also, at the very next concert-meeting, before an audience of thousands, an exchange of kisses will be arranged on the platform: the Cadet lady lecturer will kiss Breshkovskaya, Breshkovskaya will kiss ex-Minister Tsereteli, and the grateful people will therefore receive an object-lesson in republican equality, liberty and fraternity. . . .

Yes, we agree that the Cadets, Breshkovskaya and Tsereteli are in their own way devoted to democracy and are propagating it among the people. But what is to be done if our conception of democracy is somewhat different from theirs?

In our opinion, to ease the incredible burdens and miseries of the war and also to heal the terrible wounds the war

* "Cadets" means Constitutional Democrats. Breshkovskaya was a leading figure in the Socialist Revolutionary party. Tsereteli was a noted Menshevik. [Editor's Note.]

has inflicted on the people, *revolutionary democracy is needed, revolutionary* measures of the kind described in the example of the distribution of housing accommodation in the interests of the poor. *Exactly the same* procedure must be adopted in both town and country for the distribution of provisions, clothing, footwear, etc., in respect of the land in the rural districts, and so forth. For the administration of the state in *this* spirit we can *at once set in motion a state* apparatus consisting of ten if not twenty million people, an apparatus such as no capitalist state has ever known. We alone can create such an apparatus, for we are sure of the fullest and devoted sympathy of the vast majority of the population. We alone can create such an apparatus, because we have class-conscious workers disciplined by by long capitalist "schooling" (it was not for nothing that we went to learn in the school of capitalism), workers who are *capable* of forming a workers' militia and of *gradually* expanding it (beginning to expand it at once) into a militia *embracing the whole people*. The class-conscious workers must lead, but for the work of administration they can enlist the vast mass of the working and oppressed people.

It goes without saying that this new apparatus is bound to make mistakes in taking its first steps. But did not the peasants make mistakes when they emerged from serfdom and began to manage their own affairs? Is there any way other than practice by which the people can learn to govern themselves and to avoid mistakes? Is there any way other than by proceeding immediately to genuine self-government by the people? The chief thing now is to abandon the prejudiced bourgeois-intellectualist view that only special officials, who by their very social position are entirely dependent upon capital, can administer the state. The chief thing is to put an end to the state of affairs in which bourgeois officials and "socialist" ministers are trying to govern in the old way, but are incapable of doing so and, after seven months, are faced with a peasant revolt in a peasant country! The chief thing is to imbue the oppressed and the working people with confidence in their own strength, to prove to them in practice that they can and must themselves ensure the *proper*, most strictly regulated and organised distribution of bread, all kinds of food, milk, clothing, housing, etc., *in the interests of the poor*. Unless this is done, Russia *cannot* be saved from collapse and ruin. The conscientious, bold, universal move to hand over administrative work to proletarians and semi-proletarians, will, however, rouse such unprecedented revolutionary enthusiasm among the people, will so multiply the people's forces in combating distress, that much that seemed impossible to our narrow, old, bureaucratic forces will become possible for the millions, who will *begin to work for themselves* and not for the capitalists, the gentry, the bureaucrats, and not out of fear of punishment.

Pertinent to the question of the state apparatus is also the question of centralism raised with unusual vehemence and ineptitude by Comrade Bazarov in *Novaya Zhizn* No. 138, of September 27, in an article entitled: "The Bolsheviks and the Problem of Power."

Comrade Bazarov reasons as follows: "The Soviets are not an apparatus suitable for all spheres of state life," for, he says, seven months' experience has shown, and "scores and hundreds of documents in the possession of the Economic Department of the St. Petersburg Executive Committee" have confirmed, that the Soviets, although actually enjoying "full power" in many places, "have not been able to achieve anything like satisfactory results in combating economic ruin." What is needed is an apparatus "divided up according to branches of production, with strict centralisation within each branch, and subordinated to one, country-wide centre." "It is a matter," if you please, "not of replacing the old apparatus, but merely of reforming it . . . no matter how much the Bolsheviks may jeer at people with a plan. . . ."

All these arguments of Comrade Bazarov's are positively amazing for their helplessness, they echo the arguments of the bourgeoisie and reflect their class point of view.

In fact, to say that the Soviets have anywhere in Russia ever enjoyed "full power" is simply ridiculous (if it is not a repetition of the selfish class lie of the capitalists). Full power means power over all the land, over all the banks, over all the factories; a man who is at all familiar with the facts of history and science on the connection between politics and economics could not have "forgotten" this "trifling" circumstance.

The bourgeoisie's device is to *withhold* power from the Soviets, *sabotage* every important step they take, while at the same time retaining government in their own hands, retaining power over the land, the banks, etc., and then throwing the blame for the ruin upon the Soviets! This was exactly the whole sad experience of the [Provisional Government].

The Soviets have never had full power, and the measures they have taken could not result in anything but palliatives that added to the confusion.

The effort to prove the necessity for centralism to the Bolsheviks who are centralists by conviction, by their programme and by the entire tactics of their Party, is really like forcing an open door. The writers of *Novaya Zhizn* are wasting their time only because they have totally failed to understand the meaning and significance of our jeers at their "country-wide" point of view. And the *Novaya Zhizn* people have failed to understand this because they merely pay *lip-service* to the doctrine of the class struggle, but do not accept it seriously. Repeating the words about the class struggle they have learned by rote, they are constantly slipping into the "above-class point of view," amusing in theory and reactionary in practice, and are calling this fawning upon the bourgeoisie a "country-wide" plan.

The state, dear people, is a class concept. The state is an organ or instrument of violence exercised by one class against another. So long as it is an instrument of violence exercised by the bourgeoisie against the proletariat, the proletariat can have only one slogan: *destruction* of this state. But when the state will be a proletarian state, when it will be an instrument of violence exercised by the proletariat against the bourgeoisie, we shall be fully and unreservedly in favour of a strong state power and of centralism.

To put it in more popular language, we do not jeer at "plans," but at Bazarov and Co.'s failure to understand that by repudiating "workers' control," by repudiating the "dictatorship of the proletariat" they *are for* the dictatorship of the bourgeoisie. There is no middle course; a middle course is the futile dream of the petty-bourgeois democrat.

Not a single central body, not a single Bolshevik has ever argued against *centralisation* of the Soviets, against their amalgamation. None of us objects to having factory committees in each branch of production, or to their centralisation. Bazarov is *wide of the mark*.

We laugh, have laughed, and will laugh not at "centralism," and not at "plans," but at *reformism*, because, after the experience of the coalition, your reformism is utterly ridiculous. And to say "not replace the apparatus but reform it" means to be a reformist, means to become not a revolutionary but a reformist democrat. Reformism means nothing more than concessions on the part of the ruling class, but *not* its overthrow; it makes concessions, but power remains in *its hands*.

This is precisely what has been tried during six months of the coalition.[2]

This is what we laugh at. Having failed to obtain a thorough grasp of the doctrine of the class struggle, Bazarov allows himself to be caught by the bourgeoisie who sing in chorus "Just so, just so, we are by no means opposed to reform, we are in favour of the workers participating in country-wide control, we fully agree with that," and good Bazarov *objectively* sings the descant for the capitalists.

This has always been and always will be the case with people who in the thick

of intense class struggle want to take up a "middle" position. And it is because the writers of *Novaya Zhizn* are incapable of understanding the class struggle that their policy is such a ridiculous and eternal oscillation between the bourgeoisie and the proletariat.

Get busy on "plans," dear citizens, that is not politics, that is not the class struggle; here you may be of use to the people. You have many economists on your paper. Unite with those engineers and others who are willing to work on problems of regulating production and distribution; devote the centre page of your big "apparatus" (your paper) to a practical study of precise facts on the production and distribution of goods in Russia, on banks, syndicates, etc., etc. —that is how you will be of use to the people; that is how your sitting between two stools will not be particularly harmful; such work on "plans" will earn not the ridicule, but the gratitude of the workers.

When the proletariat is victorious it will do the following, it will set economists, engineers, agronomists, and so forth, to work *under the control* of the workers' organisations on drawing up a "plan," on verifying it, on devising labour-saving methods of centralisation, on devising the simplest, cheapest, most convenient and universal measures and methods of control. For this we shall pay the economists, statisticians and technicians good money . . . but we shall not give them anything to eat if they do not perform this work conscientiously and entirely *in the interests of the working people*.

We are in favour of centralism and of a "plan," but of the centralism and plan of the *proletarian* state, of proletarian regulation of production and distribution in the interests of the poor, the working people, the exploited, *against* the exploiters. We can agree to only one meaning of the term "country-wide," namely, that which breaks the resistance of the capitalists, which gives all power to the majority of the people, i.e., the proletarians and semiproletarians, the workers and the poor peasants.

---

[2] Lenin refers to the Provisional Government coalition of socialists and nonsocialists. [Editor's note.]

Leon Trotsky

GENIAL SHAPER OF SOVIET POWER

Leon Trotsky's most notable works were written after Stalin, having engineered his expulsion from the Communist Party in 1927, compelled him two years later to abandon Soviet territory and go into exile. Systematically maligned by the party apparatus and accused of having always been opposed to Lenin on all basic political issues, Trotsky's autobiography and his *History of the Russian Revolution* tend to overrate the extent to which he and Lenin, although never close personal friends, collaborated harmoniously as political leaders. In these works Trotsky seems especially concerned with proving that he and Lenin shared ideas in the period 1917 to 1921, when their names jointly stood for the great victories won in the name of the revolution. The passage below, however, is drawn from the fragmentary biography of Lenin that Trotsky pulled together from memories of a quarter of a century shortly after Lenin's death in 1924. Although eulogistic in tone, Trotsky's writing at this point did not yet have to prove the author's spiritual union with the departed leader and can, therefore, be regarded as a generally objective account.

FORMING THE GOVERNMENT

THE power in Petersburg was won. Therefore it was a question of forming the government.

"What name shall we use?" Lenin considered aloud. "Not minister, that is a repulsive, worn-out designation."

"We might say commissars," I suggested, "but there are too many commissars now. Perhaps chief commissar. . . . No, 'chief' sounds bad. What about people's commissars?" . . .

"People's Commissars? As for me, I like it. And the government as a whole?"

"Council of People's Commissars?"

"Council of People's Commissars," Lenin repeated. "That is splendid. That smells of revolution."

I remember this last expression literally. . . .

Every one who knows anything about Lenin knows very well that one of his strongest sides was the ability to separate the essence of a thing from its form.

But this does not contradict in any way the fact that he valued the form also extraordinarily, for he knew the power of the formal on the mind, and thereby changed the formal into the material. From the moment that the Provisional Government was overthrown Lenin officiated as the government in large things as well as small. We had as yet no apparatus; connection with the country was lacking; the employees were on strike; Wikshel* cut the telephone connection with Moscow; we had neither money nor an army. But Lenin took hold of absolutely everything by means of statutes, decrees, and commands in the name of the government. Naturally he was further removed than any one from a superstitious adherence to formal oaths. He had recognized too clearly that our power lay in the new state apparatus which was built up by the masses, by

* All-Russian Executive Committee of Railway Workers Union. [Editor's note.]

From Leon Trotsky, *Lenin* (New York: Minton, Balch and Company, 1925), pp. 132–151.

the Petrograd districts. But to combine the work coming from above, from the abandoned or wrecked government offices, with the productive work from below, this tone of formal energy was necessary, the tone of a government that to-day is a mere idea, but to-morrow or the day after will be the power and consequently must act to-day as the power. . . .

"They," said Lenin speaking of the enemy, "are faced by the danger of losing everything. And moreover they have hundreds of thousands of men who have gone through the school of war, sated, determined, officers ready for anything, ensigns, bourgeois, and heirs of land owners, police and well-to-do peasants. And there are, pardon the expression, 'revolutionaries' who imagine we should complete the revolution in love and kindness. Yes? Where did they go to school? What do they understand by dictatorship? What will become of a dictatorship if one is a weakling?"

We heard such tirades from him a dozen times a day and they were always aimed at some one among those present who was suspected of "pacifism." Lenin let no opportunity pass, when they spoke in his presence of the revolution and the dictatorship, particularly if this happened at the meetings of the Council of People's Commissars, or in the presence of the Left Social Revolutionaries or hesitating Communists, of remarking: "Where have we a dictatorship? Show it to me. It is confusion we have, but no dictatorship."

The word "confusion" he was very fond of. "If we are not ready to shoot a saboteur and white guardist, what sort of big revolution is that? Just see how the bourgeois pack writes about us in the press! Where is there a dictatorship here? Nothing but talk and confusion. . . ." These speeches expressed his actual feeling, but at the same time they had a twofold end: according to his method Lenin hammered into the heads the consciousness that only unusually strong measures could save the revolution.

The weakness of the new state apparatus was most clearly manifest at the moment the Germans began the attack. "Yesterday we still sat firm in the saddle," said Lenin when alone with me, "and today we are only holding fast to the mane. But it is also a lesson. And this lesson cannot fail to have an effect upon our cursed negligence. To create order and really to attack the thing, is what we must do, if we do not wish to be enslaved! It will be a very good lesson if . . . if only the Germans, along with the Whites, do not succeed in overthrowing us."

"Well," Vladimir Ilyich once asked me quite unexpectedly, "if the White Guards kill you and me will Bucharin come to an understanding with Sverdlof?"

"Perhaps they will not kill us," I answered jokingly.

*　　*　　*

The government, which was renewed rather often in its separate parts, developed a feverish work in decrees. Every session of the Council of People's Commissars at first presented the picture of legislative improvisation on the greatest scale. Everything had to be begun at the beginning, had to be wrung from the ground. We could not offer "precedents," for history knew of none. Even simple requests were made difficult by the lack of time. The questions came up in progression of revolutionary inquisitiveness, that is, in incredible chaos. Big and little were mingled most remarkably. Less important practical problems led to the most involved questions of principle. Not all, by no means all, the decrees were in harmony, and Lenin joked more than once, even openly, at the discords in our product of decrees. But in the end these contradictions, even if uncouth viewed from the practical tasks of the moment, were lost sight of in the work of revolutionary thinking, that, by means of legislation, pointed out new ways for a new world of human relations.

It remains to be said that the direction of this whole work was incumbent upon Lenin. He presided unweariedly, five or six hours at a time, at the Council of People's Commissars—and these meetings took place daily at the first period—

passed from question to question, led the debates, allotted the speakers' time carefully by his watch, time that was later regulated by a presiding time-meter (or second-meter).

In general the questions came up without any preparation, and they never could be postponed, as has already been stated. Very often the nature of the question, before the beginning of the debate, was unknown to the members of the Council of People's Commissars as well as to the President. But the discussions were always concise, the introductory report was given five to ten minutes. None the less the President towed the meeting into the right channel. If the meeting was well attended and if there were any specialists and particularly any unknown persons among the participants, then Vladimir Ilyich resorted to one of his favorite gestures: he put his right hand before his forehead as a shield and looked through his fingers at the reporters and particularly at the members of the assembly, by which means, contrary to the expression "to look through the fingers," he watched very sharply and attentively. On a narrow strip of paper was posted in tiny letters (economy!) the list of speakers. One eye watched the time that was posted above the table every now and then, to remind the speaker it was time to stop. At the same time the President quickly made a note of the conclusions that had seemed to him especially important in the course of the debate, in the form of resolutions. Generally, in addition to this, Lenin, to save time, sent the assembly members short memoranda in which he asked for some kind of information. These notes would represent a very voluminous and very interesting epistolary element in the technique of soviet legislation, but a large part of them has been destroyed as the answer was written on the reverse side of the note which the President then carefully destroyed. At a definite time Lenin read aloud the resolution points, that were always intentionally stiff and pedagogic— in order to emphasize, to bring into prominence, to exclude any changes; then the debates were either at an end,

or entered the concrete channel of practical motions and supplements. Lenin's "points" were thus the basis of the respective decree.

Among other necessary attributes this work required a strong creative imagination. This word may seem inadmissible at the first glance, but nevertheless it expresses exactly the essence of the thing. The human imagination may be of many kinds: the constructive engineer needs it as much as the unrestrained fiction writer. One of the most precious varieties of imagination consists in the ability to picture people, things, and phenomena as they are in reality, even when one has never seen them. The application and combination of the whole experience of life and theoretical equipment of a man with separate small stopping places caught in passing, their working up, fusion, and completion according to definite formulated laws of analogy, in order thereby to make clear a definite phase of human life in its whole concreteness—that is imagination, which is indispensable for a lawmaker, a government worker, and a leader in the time of revolution. The strength of Lenin lay, to a very important degree, in the strength of his realistic imagination.

Lenin's definiteness of purpose was always concrete,—otherwise it would have belied its name. In the "Iskra," I believe, Lenin for the first time expressed the thought, that in the complicated chain of political action one must always seek out the central link for the moment in question in order to seize it and give direction to the whole chain. Later, too, Lenin returned to this thought quite often, even to the same picture of the chain and the ring. This method passed from the sphere of the conscious, as it were, into his unconsciousness and finally became second nature. In particularly critical moments, when it was a question of a very responsible or risky tactical change of position, Lenin put aside everything else less important that permitted postponement. This must by no means be understood in the sense that he had grasped the central problem in its main features only and ignored details. Quite the contrary. He had before his eyes the problem that he considered could not be postponed, in all its concreteness, took hold of it from all sides, studied the details, now and then even the secondary ones, and sought a point of attack in order to approach it anew and give force to it,—he recalled, expounded, emphasized, controlled, and urged. But all was subordinated to the "link of the chain" which he regarded as decisive for the moment in question. He put aside, not only all that was at variance, directly or indirectly, with the central problem, but also that which might distract his attention and weaken his exertion. In particularly critical moments he was likewise deaf and blind to everything that had nothing to do with the question which held his entire interest. Merely the raising of other questions, neutral ones so to speak, he felt as a danger from which he instinctively retreated.

When one critical step had been successfully overcome, Lenin would often exclaim for some cause or another: "But we have quite forgotten to do so and so. . . . We have made a mistake while we were entirely occupied with the main problem. . . ." They often answered: "But this question came up and exactly this proposition was made, only you would not hear anything of it then."

"Yes, really?" he would reply. "I do not remember at all."

Then he laughed slily and a little "consciously" and made a peculiar motion of the hand, characteristic of him, from above below, that seemed to mean: one cannot decide everything at the same time. This "defect" was only the reverse side of his faculty of the greatest inward mobilization of all his forces, and exactly this faculty made him the greatest revolutionary of history.

In Lenin's theses about peace written in January, 1918, he says: "For the success of socialism in Russia a certain period of time of *at least a few months is necessary.*"

Now these words seem quite incomprehensible. Is it not a mistake? Are not years or decades meant? But no, it is no mistake. One could probably find a number of other statements of Lenin of the same type. I remember very well that in the first period, at the sessions of the Council of People's Commissars at Smolny, Ilyich repeatedly said that within a half year socialism would rule and that we would be the greatest state in the world. The Left Social Revolutionaries, and not alone they, raised their heads in question and surprise, regarded each other, but were silent. This was his system of inculcation. Lenin wanted to train everybody, from now on, to consider all questions in the setting of their socialistic structure, not in the perspective of the "goal," but of today and tomorrow.

In this sharp change of position he seized the method so peculiar to him, of emphasizing the extreme: Yesterday we said socialism is the goal; but today it is a question of so thinking, speaking, and acting that the rule of socialism will be guaranteed in a few months. Does that mean too that it should be only a pedagogical method? No, not that alone. To the pedagogic energy something must be added: Lenin's strong idealism, his intense will-power, that in the sudden changes of two epochs shortened the stopping places, and drew nearer to the definite ends. He *believed in what he said.* And this imaginative half-year respite for the development of socialism just as much represents a function of Lenin's spirit as his realistic taking hold of every task of today. The deep and firm conviction of the strong possibilities of human development, for which one can and must pay any price whatsoever in sacrifices and suffering, was always the mainspring of Lenin's mental structure.

Under the most difficult circumstances, in the most wearing daily work, in the midst of commissariat troubles and all others possible, surrounded by a bourgeois war, Lenin worked with the greatest care over the Soviet constitution, scrupulously harmonized minor practical requisites of the state apparatus with the problems of principle of a proletarian dictatorship in a land of peasants.

The Constitution Commission decided for some reason or other to remodel Lenin's "Declaration of the Rights of Producers" and bring it into "accord" with the text of the consti ution. When I came from the front to Mo_cow I received from the Commission, among other material, the outline of the transformed "declaration," or at least a part of it. I familiarized myself with it in Lenin's office, where only he and Sverdlof were present. They were doing the preparatory work for the Council of Soviets.

"But why is the declaration to be changed?" I asked Sverdlof, who was the head of the Constitution Commission.

Vladimir Ilyich raised his head with interest.

"Well, the Commission has just discovered that the 'declaration' contains discrepancies with the constitution and inexact formulations," Jakov Michailovich answered.

"In my opinion that is nonsense," I replied. "The declaration has already been accepted and has become an historical document—what sense is there in changing it?"

"That is quite right," Vladimir Ilyich interrupted. "I too think they have taken up this question quite unnecessarily. Let the youth live unshaven and disheveled: be he what he may, he is still a scion of the revolution . . . he will hardly be better if you send him to the barber."

Sverdlof tried "dutifully" to stand by the decision of his Commission, but he soon agreed with us. I realized that Vladimir Ilyich, who more than once had had to oppose propositions of the Constitution Commission, apparently did not wish to take up the struggle against a rearrangement of the "Declaration of the Rights of Producers," whose author he was. However, he was delighted by the support of a "third person" who unexpectedly turned up at the last moment. We three decided not to change the "declaration" and the worthy youth was spared the barber.

The study of the development of Soviet law-making in bringing into prominence its chief motives and turning points, in connection with the course of the revolution itself and the class relationships in it, presents a tremendously important task, because the results of it for the proletariat of other countries can be and must be of the greatest practical significance.

The collection of Soviet decrees forms, in a certain sense, a by no means unimportant part of the collected works of Vladimir Ilyich Lenin.

Moshe Lewin

OPPONENT OF BUREAUCRATISM

Moshe Lewin, born in Poland in 1921, worked on a collective farm in the U.S.S.R. during World War II and also served in the Red Army. He is presently Director of Studies at the École Pratique des Hautes Études in Paris. This selection from his book provides a much-needed corrective to recent trends in cold war writing that find all of the seeds of Stalinism in the deeds of Lenin. Lewin contends that although Lenin did not foresee the need for limiting the bureaucracy which was inevitable in the growth of the Soviet state, neither can Lenin be blamed for the excesses of his successor.

LENIN, who always claimed to be an orthodox Marxist, who no doubt did use the Marxist method in approaching social phenomena, and who saw the international question in class terms, approached the problems of government more like a chief executive of a strictly "elitist" turn of mind. He did not apply methods of social analysis to the government itself and was content to consider it purely in terms of organizational methods. This was simply the result of the situation of Soviet power at the beginning of 1923: political power, especially under the NEP, was practically the only instrument of action left to the Bolsheviks. This unexpected fact, which worried those who held this power, was the earliest manifestation of one of the most original characteristics of our time: the primacy of political factors, the control that governments possess over the economy and over society in general. Leninism was more apt than other schools of Marxism to grasp this truth because its voluntarism tended to emphasize political consciousness and the possibility of instilling it into the social forces from above.

Lenin's elitism, therefore, was merely an expression of his adaptation to a situation in which the driving force of the regime was an elite. His problem was how to use that elite in such a way that it would initiate the process of social transformation throughout the whole country. But in this sphere Lenin's thought contained certain weaknesses; he had failed to see the danger of the very tendencies that were soon to become so preponderant at the power summit.

It is true that in the circumstances prevailing at the end of 1921 it was quite understandable that Lenin's main concern should be the preservation of the power that had been acquired at the price of such sacrifice, rather than the organization of safeguards against the abuse of that power and against the hypertrophy of the dictatorship. The question should have occurred to him in 1922, but it escaped his attention, as did the national question, "almost completely," as he was later to admit. Lenin, who had become the prisoner of his illness, but also of his own government machine, turned at last to the difficult and perhaps in the short run insoluble problem of how to guarantee the political and moral health of the dictatorship. The social forces that should be participating effectively in its functioning could not be depended on because, first of all,

Reprinted by permission of Faber and Faber Limited and Random House, Inc. Condensed from *Lenin's Last Struggle* by Moshe Lewin, pp. 121, 126, 129–136. © Copyright 1968 by Random House, Inc.

they had to be educated. The workers, in particular, "would like to build a better apparatus for us, but they do not know how. . . . They have not yet developed the culture required for this." As for the peasants, they must themselves be watched. This was why Lenin was strongly opposed to anything that savored, however remotely, of bourgeois democracy. He might have benefitted from further thought on this matter, but in the immediate situation, any recourse to democratic practice would have soon led to the eviction of the Bolsheviks from power. So he returned to his idea of an elite, to the quality of his men, until such time as the country had acquired an adequate level of culture.

If the whole structure thus rested on an "idealist" basis, on the quality of the senior cadres, and not on the power and consciousness of the working class, this attitude, however precarious and however unexpected in a Marxist, corresponded perfectly to the situation that Lenin had to face. Later other countries were confronted with similar structural problems and attempted the same solution. In this respect, Lenin's "Testament," by proposing a policy of governmental cadres, is still of interest today. But a more extensive and deeper analysis must be made of the other aspect of the reality of power, the bureaucracy, which is a major problem for all developing countries that have chosen highly centralized and state-dominated systems.

Lenin was an ardent opponent of bureaucratism, but he did not analyze it sufficiently in depth. He admitted that as yet he did not fully understand the phenomenon: it is "a question that we have not yet been able to study." As a rule, Lenin tended to see it as an inheritance from the old regime. This explanation, while true in part, is inadequate. Moreover, the bureaucracy was to become so inextricably a part of Soviet society and so deeply entrenched in the Soviet system, because of its composition and its methods, that the elements from the past were soon to lose all importance. The explanation must be sought elsewhere.

The continual increase in the number of civil servants and in their hold on the life of the country was facilitated by a conjunction of factors inherent in a backward country that had a real need for new administrative bodies and additional administrators, if it was to develop the economy along planned, centralist lines. But this meant—and Lenin did not realize it—that the bureaucracy would become the true social basis of power. There is no such thing as "pure" political power, devoid of any social foundation. A regime must find some other social basis than the apparatus of repression itself. The "void" in which the Soviet regime had seemed to be suspended had soon been filled, even if the Bolsheviks had not seen it, or did not wish to see it. The Stalinist period might be defined, therefore, as the substitution of the bureaucracy for the original social basis of the regime, namely, the working class, a section of the poorest peasants and certain strata of the intelligentsia.

Stalin, like Lenin, was a technician of power, but lacking Lenin's intellectual and moral stature and the scruples of "the Party's European cadres," he was quite willing to incorporate into his own plans all Lenin's amendments of an idealistic, internationalist, or socialist kind, knowing that a great many things would remain on paper and that reality, as he conceived it, would gain the upper hand. Thus all the projects to which Lenin attached so much importance—the enlargement of the Central Committee, the creation of a new Central Control Commission and its fusion with the RKI[1] —would be accepted and put into practice; but since they would not be animated by the spirit in which they had been conceived, they would merely contribute to the triumph of the very tendencies Lenin wanted to combat.

If in the end Lenin's regime came to be based on a force, the bureaucracy, which he abhorred, it was only the result of a situation in which a program of development is imposed by a new regime on a backward country whose vital social forces are either weak, indifferent, or hos-

[1] Workers'-Peasants' Inspectorate. [Editor's note.]

tile. Lenin did not foresee this phenomenon because his social analysis was based on only three social classes—the workers, the peasants and the bourgeoisie—without taking any account of the state apparatus as a distinct social element in a country that had nationalized the main sectors of the economy. A great historian reproaches Lenin for not understanding the role of the administrative machine in a modern society, or rather, in a society in the process of becoming modernized. This reproach is justified to the extent that Lenin confused the bureaucratic machine with the rule of the Tsarist-type *chinovnichestvo*.[2] But he had already dealt with the question in 1918, when he came out in favor of the administration against the anarchosyndicalist tendencies of the workers; in 1923, his plans for reorganization show that he was increasingly aware of the problem.

This time he approached it from another angle. Lenin continued to analyze the Party as the "vanguard of the proletariat." But it was composed of a minority of workers, a minority moreover that did not even play the leading role, and this worried Lenin considerably. The composition of the Party reflected more or less the state of the country's social forces. At its center, as in the regime as a whole, the general tendency was to bureaucratization—which would later increase its "monolithic" character. This was particularly apparent in the preponderance of executive functions and in the pyramidal structure of the apparatus. The process was that of the transformation of a political party into a state apparatus. Stalin seized on this tendency and, instead of controlling it as Lenin wished, accepted it, based his own power upon it and developed it.

At the end of his life, Lenin saw all these problems more and more clearly, for the intention, either implicit or explicit, of all his projects was to counteract the tendencies that were appearing in the regime and would triumph after his death. He would have had to live on to prove that he could have changed anything very substantially, but in that event he would also have had to overcome certain weaknesses in his analysis and reasoning; the phenomena he speaks of in his "Testament" were not yet very clear to him.

* * *

In view of the almost negligible influence that Lenin's suggestions have actually had on events in the USSR, it might be tempting to conclude that they were merely utopian, detached from reality, or ineffective. In my opinion, they deserve more attention and a more positive appreciation. Although Lenin turned an objective eye on the problems of his regime, it is true that certain tendencies became apparent to him only at the very end of his life and others were imperfectly understood. Nevertheless, his proposals for reform represent, both in their explicit content and in their implicit consequences, a total response to the political realities of the country. . . .

Lenin was trying to establish at the summit of the dictatorship a balance between different elements, a system of reciprocal control that could serve the same function—the comparison is no more than approximate—as the separation of powers in a democratic regime. An important Central Committee, raised to the rank of Party Conference, would lay down the broad lines of policy and supervise the whole Party apparatus, while itself participating in the execution of the more important tasks, both as a body and through the activities of its individual members. Part of this Central Committee, the Central Control Commission, would, in addition to its work within the Central Committee, act as a control of the Central Committee and of its various offshoots—the Political Bureau, the Secretariat, the Orgburo. The Central Control Commission, with its specialists from the RKI or the CCC-RKI,[3] would occupy a special position with relation to the other institutions; its independence would be assured by

[2] Bureaucratic hierarchy. [Editor's note.]

[3] Central Control Commission—Workers'-Peasants' Inspectorate. [Editor's note.]

its direct link to the Party Congress, without the mediation of the Politburo and its administrative organs or of the Central Committee. Seen in this way, these projects seem complex but not very highly developed. But even if they were merely embryonic, they do acknowledge the problem of principle: how to assure the survival of a revolutionary dictatorship established in "premature" conditions and at the same time safeguard its original purity and devotion to principle. Lenin tried to rationalize the dictatorship in such a way that it could protect itself both from external enemies and from the dangers inherent in dictatorial power.

The most explicit part of Lenin's "Testament" might be summed up in these three commandments:

1. Combat nationalism, especially Russian nationalism—that Great Power chauvinism that the whole government machine tends to serve; strive to inculcate an internationalist spirit into the peoples of the Union.

2. Combat an ignorant, wasteful and potentially oppressive bureaucracy at every level, including the Party leadership; strive to create an efficient state administration.

3. Remove Stalin.

The absence, in the "Testament," of any mention of the prohibition of factions is made all the more significant by the fact that there is also no mention of terror as a means of promoting the execution of the government's plans. Terror had occupied a fairly considerable place in Lenin's earlier writings, and he had always defended it as an ultimate weapon. The new Volume XLV of the *Works* includes a number of writings that had previously been either unknown or little known in which Lenin analyzes terror as a method. It was a weapon that must always be held in reserve, Lenin reminds his readers, especially as the liberalization brought about by the NEP would tend to weaken the security of the state. In a letter to Kamenev that appeared for the first time in 1959, he declares: "It is a great mistake to think that the NEP put an end to terror; we shall again have recourse to terror and to economic terror."

He explains to Kamenev that a means must be found whereby all those who would now like to go beyond the limits assigned to businessmen by the state could be reminded "tactfully and politely" of the existence of this ultimate weapon.

But in other writings, which are more disturbing in view of the use to which they were later put, Lenin went further. In his amendments to the project for the penal code, he insisted that the notion of "counterrevolutionary activity" should be given the widest possible interpretation. This definition was to be linked with the "international bourgeoisie" in such a way that this kind of crime became quite imprecise from a juridical point of view and thus left the way wide open for every kind of arbitrary action. Among other things, the crime would cover "propaganda and agitation" and "participation in or aid to an organization" which might benefit that part of the international bourgeoisie that does not recognize the Soviet regime's equal rights with capitalist states and seeks to overthrow it by force. This definition was already broad enough, but what was worse, in view of the fact that the crime could carry capital punishment, was that it could be extended by analogy. Whoever "gave help objectively to that part of the international bourgeoisie" (which actively opposed the regime), and similarly whoever belonged to an organization within the country whose activities "might assist or be capable of assisting" this bourgeoisie, would also be guilty. This case shows that at this time Lenin was anxious to leave room for the use of terror or the threat of its use (not through the Cheka alone but through tribunals and a regular procedure) as long as the big capitalist countries continued to threaten the USSR.

Lenin, then, was very far from being a weak liberal, incapable of taking resolute action when necessary. But unlike some of his successors, he hated repression; for him, it should be used only in the defense of the regime against serious threat and as a punishment for those who contravened legality.

But to return to Lenin's last program,

the use of constraint—let alone terror—
is ostensibly excluded in establishing the
foundations of a new society. Lenin's
second *What Is To Be Done?* pleads for
caution, restraint, moderation and pa-
tience. Lenin has not abandoned the use
of constraint in the defense of the regime,
but for purposes of construction all un-
due haste is forbidden: "We must show
sound skepticism for too rapid progress,
for boastfulness, etc."—these words are
taken from "Better Fewer, But Better."[4]
"Better get good human material in two
or even three years than work in haste
without hope of getting any at all." "No
second revolution!"—this was to be the
interpretation of the "Testament" that
Bukharin, five years later, was to throw
back at Stalin, and he was right. Lenin
no longer described force as the "mid-
wife of a new society" after the seizure of
power and the return of peace; the new
rule in this new situation was clearly
that of gradual evolution. And this rule
was formulated against the whole pressure of Russian realities, which—as
Lenin was very well aware—tended in
the opposite direction.

The rule "Better fewer, but better"
would be difficult to observe, but Lenin
refuses, in advance, the argument of
spontaneous tendencies: "I know that
the opposite rule will force its way
through a thousand loopholes. I know
that enormous resistance will have to
be put up, that devilish persistence will
be required, that in the first few years
at least work in this field will be hellishly
hard. Nevertheless, I am convinced that
only by achieving this aim shall we
create a republic that is really worthy of
the name of Soviet, socialist, and so on,
and so forth."

In my opinion, one can hardly describe Lenin's great objectives as utopian.
Many of the objectives assigned to the
regime in the fields of economic and
cultural development have been attained.
The other grand design, that of creating

a dictatorial machine capable of controlling itself to a large degree, seems
closer today, but only after an initial
catastrophic failure: the Soviet regime
underwent a long period of "Stalinism,"
which in its basic features was diametri-
cally opposed to the recommendations
of the "Testament." This fact requires
some elucidation. Left-wing dictatorship
is one of the most significant political
phenomena of our time. Its role is an
important one and its prospects of development are far from exhausted. But
there is no evidence that this type of dictatorship, at a certain stage in its development, must of necessity and in every
case degenerate into a personal, despotic
and irrational dictatorship. From a historical point of view, there was nothing
essentially utopian about Lenin's aim
of achieving a rational dictatorial regime,
with men of integrity at its head and
efficient institutions working consciously
to go beyond both underdevelopment and
dictatorship. Moreover, in Lenin's own
time, and in extremely difficult conditions, the Soviet dictatorial machine still
functioned in a very different way from
the one it was later to adopt. Lenin's
plans were not put into practice because
the tendencies that had emerged from
the civil war could only be counteracted
by daring reforms, and in the absence
of a capable and undisputed leader the
plans in question remained no more than
mere "wishes." The machine that had
been set up under Lenin found no dif-
ficulty in bypassing the dead leader's
most earnest wishes; the embalming of
his corpse and the posthumous cult of
his person helped to dissimulate a type
of dictatorship utterly foreign to his
plans.

The greatest discrepancy between
Lenin's intentions and actual history is
to be found in the field of methods. It
would appear today that the USSR has
entered a period of internal development
in which economic and educative
methods are being gradually substituted
for administrative constraint, as Lenin
wished. But for a long time terror was
the main instrument in the establishment of the new structures.

---

[4] Lenin's last published article, in which he
criticized the proliferating bureaucracy and
Stalin by implication. [Editor's note.]

Alfred G. Meyer

MANIPULATOR OF THE DYNAMICS OF POWER

Alfred G. Meyer is Professor of Political Science at the University of Michigan. He previously served as Assistant Director of Harvard University's Russian Research Center and as Director of Columbia University's research program on the history of the Soviet Communist Party. He is the author of *Marxism: The Unity of Theory and Practice, Communism,* and *The Soviet Political System.* In his well-known book *Leninism,* Meyer poses a question central to an understanding of Lenin's historic role. "How much, and in what way," asks Meyer, "does the fickle support given by the masses determine the leader's action?" It is by the "concept of the revolutionary situation," Meyer explains, that "Leninism answers this question."

THE opinions and instincts of the working masses must to a certain extent guide the conscious leader, if he wants to retain his followers. In particular, the communist should not desert the masses when they do act spontaneously, even if their action is mistaken and harmful. Yet to what extent, precisely, should the masses be followed? How much influence should the conscious leader give to the unenlightened thoughts and actions of the common man? How much, and in what way, does the fickle support given by the masses determine the leader's action?

Leninism answers this question by the concept of the revolutionary situation. There are certain moments when a society is ripe for revolutionary action. These moments are determined by the social conditions and by the mood of the masses. The presumption in Leninism is that whenever objective conditions are ripe for revolution, the spontaneous will to action of the masses will also be at the highest point of its development. Yet it is admitted that the mood of the masses may at times be out of tune with actual developments. In any event, it is up to the conscious leaders to assess the strength of both, weigh them against each other, and on the basis of this diagnosis choose the most propitious moment for action. The moment should not be too late, for then the enthusiasm of the masses may have spent itself. Nor must it be too early: "If we speak about civil war before people have grasped its necessity, then doubtless we fall into the error of Blanquism." And the ability to make such an appraisal is one of the necessary qualifications of a truly conscious revolutionary leader. "The art of the politician, and the correct understanding by the communist of his own tasks, consists in the correct appraisal of the conditions and the moment when the vanguard of the proletariat can successfully seize power; when it will be able, during and after this, to obtain sufficient support from sufficiently broad sections of the working class and the nonproletarian working masses; when he will, after that, be able to support, strengthen, and broaden his rule, educating, teaching, and attracting wider and wider masses of the laboring population."

Marxism in its original form maintained that the spontaneous unfolding of historical events produces progress and, finally, a rationally acceptable form of human relations. Leninism is more pessimistic and therefore became a manipulative theory of history. Its aim is to subject the most irrational, spontaneous forces to reason (consciousness) by means of organization; even revolution is made the object of science and rational organization. Yet the irrational forces are recognized as given, and they receive their place in the rationalized scheme of revolution. Their specific function is to help determine the moment of action. . . .

In short, revolution, according to Lenin, can not be the work of conspirators alone; it must be made by an entire people or by an overwhelming majority. Moreover, during a revolution initiative almost inevitably goes to the masses, at least for a while. This is precisely the meaning of the revolutionary situation: the masses have taken the initiative, or are about to take it. It is the test of an able revolutionary leader to make use of these "elemental forces" and ride to power on the waves of spontaneity.

To be sure, Lenin emphasized that these elemental forces which make the wheels of history turn must never be allowed to engulf and overwhelm conscious leadership. Spontaneity must never be permitted to change the direction of the party's action, the party line. And yet, when it becomes necessary in the interests of the power struggle, the party must follow mass opinion even if it means breaking with its own platform. This was Lenin's argument at least in 1917, at the time of the October Revolution, when he rode his party to power on the waves of mass enthusiasm for slogans to which the Bolsheviks subscribed for purely opportunistic reasons. "The vast majority of peasants, soldiers, and workers are in favor of a policy of peace," explained Lenin. "This is not the policy of the Bolsheviks; it is not a 'party' policy at all; but it is the policy of the workers, soldiers, and peasants, that is, of the majority of the people. We are not carrying out the program of the Bolsheviks, and in agrarian matters our program has been taken entirely from the mandates of the peasants."

In this and subsequent instances Lenin went further in "submitting to spontaneity" than was acceptable to some of his party comrades, and he was therefore accused of becoming an opportunist who was allowing the party to get stuck in the morass of public opinion. By following the masses, they argued, the party was descending to their level, instead of lifting them up. Lenin's reply was that the danger of following spontaneity was, of course, very great. Mass unrest is a tricky ally; yet it must be used by the conscious leadership, and the more courageously the better. For only a courageous leader can ride the waves of mass opinion and tame them. They are the element he needs in order to act. The element is treacherous, but without it the revolutionary is paralyzed. "Do not fear the initiative and independence of the masses! Entrust yourselves to their revolutionary organization—and you will see in *all* areas of political affairs the same force, grandeur, and invincibility that the workers and peasants showed in their unity and passion against the Kornilov affair." Moreover, the conscious vanguard not only makes use of mass spontaneity, but also serves to check it by taking the masses in hand: "otherwise the wave of real anarchy may become stronger than we are." If the party were to be destroyed or silenced, the masses would continue to react to the misery of their status; but they would react spontaneously, that is, in a nonrational and hence purely destructive manner. "Where Bolshevism has the possibility of coming out in the open, there will be no disorganization. But where there are no Bolsheviks, or where they are prevented from speaking up, there will be excesses, there will be decay, there will be pseudo-Bolsheviks."

In short, spontaneity, though it is essential to the revolution, must be used judiciously. The spontaneous instincts and actions of the masses are the natural element available to the conscious social scientist, but spontaneity is of use to him only if it is harnessed, transformed into political energy, and channeled into the most advantageous direction. Then it is welcomed, and the more there is of it the better it is for the professional revolutionary. . . .

While it is true that in the main [Lenin] denied rationality to the workingman, he did not maintain this attitude unhesitatingly. On the contrary, he more than once allowed himself to be led astray by an unusually optimistic appraisal of proletarian consciousness. Lenin was thus torn between two judgments about the working class. In tracing the ups and downs of his estimate of proletarian rationality, we find that his opinion becomes optimistic as soon as the masses begin to engage in spontaneous revolutionary action, following the slogans preached by himself and his associates. Conversely, as soon as the masses cease to obey the commands or suggestions of the party, his estimate of their consciousness declines sharply. Lenin thus was caught in the same dilemma in which modern democratic theorists find themselves; and in being one of the first men to voice doubts in working-class consciousness, he is one of the pathbreakers of contemporary political thought. In theories of democracy, the rationality of the "common man" is as indispensable a premise as the workers' class consciousness is in Marxism. Although Lenin's faith in it was shaken, he never completely abandoned it because then he would have had to abandon his entire ideology. Somewhere, at some point, his theories inevitably assume that workers will acquire consciousness. Similarly, all ideas of democracy collapse once the faith in the common man's rationality is abandoned. Yet we are even less sure of it than was Lenin, whose lack of faith was based only on political horse sense, whereas ours is intensified by the incontrovertible findings of psychology and anthropology. Democratic theorists of our day are therefore as schizophrenic with regard to this problem as the Leninists, and only those who have no scruples in abandoning democracy as an ideal wholeheartedly accept all evidence about man's alienation and project it into the indefinite future.

The problem of working-class consciousness has an important implication for the party: the leaders must ask themselves how much sense it makes to engage in political action without fully conscious support. In particular, how much sense does it make, in terms of Marxist schemes and theories, to seize power before the working class is fully conscious? In the Marxist movement, it had been considered axiomatic that action should be consonant with the development of consciousness. Hence Marxists believed it senseless, irresponsible, or even criminal to undertake revolutionary action, much less think of socialism, before true consciousness was developed among the working class. Lenin did not take a definite stand in opposition to this. True, he denied consciousness to the proletariat; yet he claimed that his party was to remedy this situation by educating the working class, and, as we have just seen, he more than once convinced himself that the task had been accomplished, that the masses were enlightened.

At least he felt it necessary to pretend that such was his conviction, in order to counter Menshevik criticism that the party had engaged in irresponsible adventurism. In reality, Lenin was prepared to take action before the masses were ready for it. Confident that, with the progressive development of capitalism, the proletariat would inevitably come to identify socialism with its own class interests, the moderate socialists favored postponing revolutionary action until the workers had acquired class consciousness. Lenin, on the other hand, appeared impatient with the development of this consciousness and held that waiting for it would mean betraying the revolution. The essence of Marxism, for him, was not the morphology of events outlined by Marx, according to which capitalism was to be transformed into socialism, but rather the consciousness of the inevitable necessity of this transformation, and the desire to achieve it as quickly as possible, by whatever means might be available in a given society. In other words, Marxism was not so much a scheme of historical development as the recognition of the direction in which history was moving and of the historical tasks facing the twentieth century, combined with a method of solving historical problems by means of the class struggle. He could, therefore, concede that the proletariat by itself would never attain anything but trade-union consciousness, thus justifying the educating role of the enlightened intellectuals; he could even become impatient with the educational process and condemn excessive reliance on it as a betrayal of the revolution; yet impatience did not necessarily lead him to despair of the creation of a socialist society, as it would have led a Menshevik or other defenders of constitutional democratism. Lenin, in seeking to bring about the revolution, was satisfied with mass support acquired by nonrational means. The development of true consciousness among the proletariat could come later, under the well-established dictatorship of the conscious vanguard. In the meantime, the problem of power was paramount, and this problem could be solved by relying on the spontaneous support of the masses, generated if necessary by propaganda.

In Leninist writings the issue is seldom posed as clearly as this. The belief that a conscious vanguard is required to lead the revolution is expressed simultaneously with confidence in the proletariat. This confidence leads to the firm conviction, often voiced by Lenin and his followers, that the workers, though not conscious, will nonetheless join forces with the vanguard and let themselves be guided by it. Yet, if it is indeed true that the workers are blinded by narrow economic interests, why should they be expected to recognize the identity of their ultimate goals with those of the conscious vanguard? Must they not be conscious already in order to remain faithful to the party at all times? Like the Hobbesian concept of the individuals' submission to leviathan, the proletariat's voluntary subordination of its own narrowly conceived class interests to the higher interests of the movement as a whole can be explained only as a rational

decision. The worker, if he is to submit to leviathan, must be wholly conscious already. That he cannot be so, Leninism takes for granted. Hence it requires irrational incentives, such as coercion and propaganda, to make the proletariat submit to the conscious elite.

Because Lenin was loath to see this conclusion clearly, the meaning of the word "consciousness" came to be weakened considerably in his spoken and written pronouncements. At times he and his friends seem to have believed that spontaneous feelings of resentment would gradually transform themselves into true consciousness, and there is a persistent tendency to hail these spontaneous feelings themselves as consciousness. What is even more remarkable is that the word "consciousness" was often used simply to denote the workers' acceptance of the vanguard's leadership and of their own humble role as rank-and-file soldiers of the revolution, regardless of how this acceptance had been generated. Hence even mass support acquired by irrational means of persuasion was often regarded as an indication of the consciousness of the masses. This self-deception was necessary whenever Lenin wished to reassure himself concerning the common man's rationality; it was equally necessary as a justification for radical action by the party. Lenin's impatient radicalism and his conviction that he had the masses squarely behind him mutually supported each other.[1]

---

[1] Thus in 1917 Lenin was convinced that he had the masses behind him because they were in conscious agreement with his aims: "If they tell us the Bolsheviks have thought out some sort of utopian story like the introduction of socialism in Russia, and that this is an impossible thing, then we answer: but in what way could the sympathy of the majority of the workers, peasants, and soldiers have been drawn to the side of utopians and dreamers?" (Lenin, vol. 22, p. 236). See also the conclusion he drew from the success of the October Revolution: "The first task of any party of the future is to convince the majority of the people of the correctness of its program and tactics. . . . Today that task, which of course is still far from completion and can never be fully exhausted, has in the main been solved; for the majority of workers and peasants in Russia . . . are certainly on the side of the Bolsheviks" (vol. 22, p. 441). . . .
Lenin frequently obtained overly optimistic

Yet every time Lenin deceived himself in this manner, the subsequent development of mass opinion disappointed him further, and strengthened anew his conviction that the vanguard was needed to lead the common man. Each manifestation of mass support for the party was hailed as a growth of the workers' consciousness; each subsequent manifestation of mass resistance to the party confirmed his secret conviction that the workingman was forever locked in the fetters of capitalist modes of thought and would have to be liberated by force. Pending his liberation from the bonds of false consciousness, however, the workingman's support of the party had to be assured by nonrational means, because he himself would have to act to free himself.[2] Thus each optimistic appraisal of the workers' consciousness led Lenin to greater contempt of the common man's rationality. Ultrademocratic leanings went hand in hand with elitist practices.[3]

---

conclusions concerning the consciousness of the masses from a corresponding overestimation of the enemy's class consciousness. By ascribing well-developed class consciousness to non-Leninists, he could thus consider every victory over them as a token of the growth of true consciousness in the proletariat.

[2] In a speech given in May 1919, Lenin frankly criticized those who insisted on the fulfillment of the "campaign" promises of 1917, calling them deceivers of the people and enemies of the Soviet regime. The promises on which his party rode to power, he claimed, had catered only to the opinions of the masses, not to true consciousness; and such promises do not count. The speech was entitled, "On the Deception of the People by Slogans of Liberty and Equality" (Lenin, vol. 24, pp. 279–383). "Just because the revolution has started," he wrote earlier, "the people have not turned into saints" (vol. 23, p. 186; translation in A Letter to American Workers, New York, 1934, p. 19).

[3] It should be remembered that a similar ambivalence characterized the thought of Marx, who in theory extolled the rationality of the proletariat, but in the privacy of his study expressed doubts about it. The difference between his case and Lenin's was that the latter incorporated these doubts in his theories even though he never entirely abandoned his faith in the workers' consciousness. In Lenin's writings the dilemma is therefore expressed more openly. Incidentally, his doubts of the workers' rationality must be contrasted with his emotional attachment to proletarians as actual human beings, the fact that he was a master at winning over working-class audiences and felt comfortable only in the company of workers and other simple folk. In this he was noticeably unlike Marx.

This ambiguity can be traced also in another set of Leninist ideas, namely, the conception of the party's task in bringing consciousness to the workingman. As long as "consciousness" is considered to be tantamount to rational, scientific judgment, the party's task is an educational one. But when the word is used in the sense of the mere readiness to follow the party's orders, the task is one of manipulating the masses.

It is clear that any choice between education and manipulation is decided by the educator's faith in his pupils' ability to absorb and use the knowledge, doctrine, and method that may be given them. The educator imparts his truths in order to influence the minds and actions of his pupils and to give them certain standards of behavior, of whose utility and expedience he is convinced. He desires to shape men in his own image. If he believes that the pupils have the ability to arrive at these standards of behavior by the same intellectual path he himself trod, he will educate. In such measure as he lacks that faith, he will be tempted to use manipulative means to make his charges behave in the desired manner.

One form of manipulation is the influencing of minds by nonrational messages of communication, customarily called propaganda. An individual educates as long as he imparts to his students that information and that scientific method which he himself is convinced are most nearly true. He propagandizes when he gives out information or teaches methods that are a distortion, misrepresentation, or contradiction of what he is convinced is most nearly true. In other words, the distinction between education and propaganda is a subjective one, and reflects the educator's confidence in the student's ability to learn.

Leninist terminology tends to confuse us here, for what we have called "education" Lenin called "propaganda," using the word in the same way as missionaries of the church speak of "propagating the faith." What we have called "propaganda," Lenin calls "agitation." Agitation to him denotes the activity of inciting the masses to action by playing on their instincts and passions, whereas propaganda in his vocabulary refers to the educational activity of spreading the communist doctrine and method; its aim is to make its recipients truly conscious. Lenin has made his distinction between the two words quite clear:

A propagandist, when he discusses unemployment, must explain the capitalist nature of the crisis; he must show the reason for its inevitability in modern society; he must describe the necessity of rebuilding society on a socialist basis, and so on. In a word, he must give many ideas all together, so many that all of them will not be understood by the average person, and in their totality they will be understood by relatively few. The agitator, on the other hand, will pick out one more or less familiar and concrete aspect of the entire problem, let us say, the death of an unemployed worker as a result of starvation. His efforts will be concentrated on this fact, in order to impart to the masses a single idea—the idea of the senseless contradiction between the growth of wealth and the growth of poverty. He will strive to evoke among the masses discontent and revolt against this great injustice and will leave the full explanation of this contradiction to the propagandist.

The characteristic form of agitation, as perfected by Lenin, is the political slogan, a simplified form of communication that can be used not only to impart knowledge but also to arouse the masses to action and familiarize them with the party, again in as direct and concrete a fashion as possible. Lenin's wife tells of the origin of a typical slogan:

When the party program was being discussed at the Second Congress, Vladimir Ilyich proposed, and strongly defended, the slogan of returning to the peasants the "pieces" of land that were cut off from them in the reform of 1861.
It seemed to him that in order to attract the peasantry it would be necessary to advocate a concrete demand corresponding as closely as possible with the needs of the peasantry. In exactly the same way as the social democrats began their agitation among the workers with the fight for hot water, for reduction of working hours, for punctual payment of wages, so the peasantry had to be organized around a concrete slogan.

It is interesting to note how the words "to organize" crept into a paragraph about agitation. The reason is that organization is but another method of manipulation; and nothing perhaps was of greater interest to Lenin than this means of influencing the masses. Lenin conceived of the proletarian revolution as the product of great minds, who, conscious of inexorable trends, would create order and progress out of chaotic elements by organizing the raw material of history in a rational fashion. His deep sympathies for the working class were rationalized by the fact that it lent itself most ideally for such organization by the conscious vanguard. Marx had considered the proletariat the Chosen People because, thrust into inhuman conditions, it had been so alienated from its humanity that it could speak for tortured mankind as such; it had been so completely cast out of human society that it would be totally opposed to the existing order and could therefore overthrow it. In Lenin's eyes, on the other hand, the proletariat is the chief instrument of conscious history-makers because it can be awakened from its political stupor into action. Most important, however, the working class had been already organized in the modern machine shop; it had been organized by its life in the big city's tenement districts. It would therefore lend itself to even more deliberate organization on a national scale, and this would permit the centralization of the revolutionary effort in the hands of a national general staff.

Lenin throughout his life was intensely preoccupied with problems of organization. His aim was to perfect the instrument of revolution-making into a machinery (*apparat*) that could be used effectively as the generals of the revolution might see fit to use it. He thought of the party as an institution in which rationality had taken concrete form as a mighty historical force. The secret of its strength would lie in the fact that the party was to act as an organization through which consciousness could get hold of the masses. It was to be a sort of transmission belt for imparting the will of the leaders to the rank and file of the followers and fellow travelers. The party apparat would enable the leadership to make the masses act whenever the wires of organization were pulled. For organization always has a purpose, and where the party would do the organizing, or acquire a hold over the organization, the purposes would be determined by its leaders. It is therefore often possible, in discussing Leninism, to use the terms "organization" and "propaganda" (in the customary sense) interchangeably.

Lenin developed the concept of what we today call the front organization. The party should not only have leaders and rank-and-file followers; it should in addition develop a sort of open superstructure, an appended network of mass organizations, undogmatic, elastic in the way they were organized and in the activities they pursued, sensitive to the shifting requirements of local and temporary conditions, but firmly guided in whatever they were doing by the party's leaders. We perceive here the first conception of totalitarian politics: Lenin seems to have envisaged an ideal situation, in which the whole of society would be converted into a network of front organizations, and the entire organizational and associational life of the country would be guided by the conscious leadership, through its control of the apparat.

The party as conceived by Lenin is therefore far more than a conspiratorial group of Marxist intellectuals. It is of necessity a dual organization of leaders and followers, or rather, a system of organizations grouped in concentric rings around the conscious leadership: "The smallest possible number of the most homogeneous possible groups should lead the movement, past masters in the business of professional revolution-making. The greatest possible number of the most diverse and heterogeneous groups from the most various layers of the proletariat (and of the other classes of the people as well) should participate in the movement." There is, of course, no question in Lenin's mind that the conscious leaders are the most valuable part of the movement. Not only is it vital that they remain ideologically sound and retain real leadership in the party, but it is also clear to Lenin that they are less expendable than any other group. Hence in times of trouble, when the class struggle goes against the proletariat or when the consciousness of the masses is at a very low ebb, Lenin's chief concern is to retain the nucleus intact. The proletarian armies may desert, but the general staff must remain. For even if the mass basis vanishes temporarily, the preservation of the central organization will guarantee the ultimate victory of the proletarian cause.

Nonetheless we cannot characterize Lenin's party adequately by contrasting its small nucleus of professional revolutionaries to the mass party envisioned by the Mensheviks. Leninism, too, required a mass basis; indeed, it was much more skilled and successful than the Mensheviks in organizing the masses for its own purposes. The difference lies in the manner in which the masses were to be recruited and organized, in the relationship between leaders and followers, and in the sociological composition of the highest leadership cadres, not in the fact that one or the other branch of Russian Marxism was more eager for mass support.

In short, although Lenin at times denounced manipulative methods, his general tendency was to be impatient with the working class. He felt that there was no time to make the masses conscious; instead, they had to be organized. "The habits of the capitalist system are too strong; the task of re-educating a people educated in these habits for centuries is a difficult job which demands a lot of time. But we say: Our fighting method is organization. We must organize everything, take everything into our own hands, ..." Social forces are there to be used by the conscious history-maker. Spontaneity is something that can be manipulated. Hence his insistence on organization, discipline, central direction, and leadership.

At the same time Lenin tended to deceive himself concerning the novelty of this approach by constantly obscuring the difference between education and manipulation, between conviction and constraint. The reason is that, for him, agitation and manipulation were but part of the educational work. The party leader manipulating the masses through the transmission belts of organization was only to goad them into acting rationally. The agitator whose task was to arouse the masses to anger and action was not to tell lies but merely to simplify the truth. This simplified truth, the slogan, was not intended to deceive the proletariat; it functioned as a sort of political shorthand, necessitated by the presumably limited understanding of the workers. The aim of slogans and of agitation in general was to awaken the workers, and this awakening was meant to be but the first step in their education for consciousness. It is therefore not astonishing that Lenin used the terms "education" and "propaganda" interchangeably. Since in his opinion education meant the inculcation of Marxist doctrine, the term "communist propaganda" became synonymous with the term "education." There are passages in his works where he seems to draw a distinction between them, for instance, when he told the Eighth Congress of Soviets that "the dictatorship of the proletariat was successful because it knew how to combine coercion and conviction."[4] Yet, from the context, it seems very likely that both these terms as they are used here refer only to manipulation.

According to Marxist theory, communism denotes a certain state of mind,

even a change in human nature, which is according to Leninism, facilitated by education. The primary educational instrument, wrote Lenin, must be the "force of example." This would work, for instance, in a situation where the masses out of habit or force of tradition stubbornly retained outmoded methods of production. If the party were to take the initiative in setting up model organizations or creating more efficient methods, the success of these new ways would force the most stubborn traditionalist to adopt them. Lenin, in speaking of the "force of example," remarked that it was basically a method of *moral* persuasion. Yet if it did not work, he continued, it should be backed up by *coercive* "persuasion." The "force of example" is thus clearly a mixture of coercion and education.

We have seen that Lenin confused the effects of education and manipulation by giving the term "consciousness" a wide and ambiguous meaning; it came to denote any willingness on the part of the workers to follow the commands of the party. Hence he failed to distinguish between genuine public opinion and opinions fabricated by the vanguard, and was sharply disappointed whenever the masses deserted their leaders, and manipulation was resorted to.

In the actual development of the party's relation to the Russian working class, this reliance on manipulation as a short cut to success in revolution had ominous consequences. So long as manipulation was used, the process of education could not go on. The original mission of the vanguard, that of raising the masses to consciousness, tended to be forgotten because of the more immediate problem of keeping the party in power. Manipulation tended to replace education altogether. The possession of power requires a continual appraisal of public opinion, and yet the manipulative methods which seek to mold that opinion tend to blind the rulers themselves to the actual trends. The stress on manipulation, utilizing means in which coercion played a conspicuous role, resulted in making brutal suppression of criticism seem to be an easier way of staying in

---

[4] Lenin, vol. 26, p. 32. When Lenin tells communist school teachers that "the task of the new education is to tie the work of teaching in with the tasks of the socialist organization of society" (vol. 23, p. 66), the careful reader will be at a loss to say with certainty whether this education is to teach skills to the masses so that they learn how to work with modern machinery, whether it is to persuade them to accept the dictatorship of the party and have confidence in a better future, or whether Lenin had in mind the creation of a new collectivist man, the education of the masses to genuine consciousness. Most probably Lenin, if asked about this, would have said that education in Soviet society would comprise all of these aspects.

power than a sensitive and careful incorporation of mass opinion into public policy-making.

The vanguard's initial lack of confidence in the workers doubtless tended to widen the gulf of mutual misunderstanding by making the workers react to events in an increasingly less rational or enlightened fashion, and this in turn increased the leaders' initial contempt of public opinion. A vicious circle of education and manipulation led to the inevitable defeat of all efforts at educating the common man to consciousness. What made the circle vicious was the problem of power, coupled with the Leninists' impatient refusal to wait for "history to take care of itself."

SUGGESTIONS FOR ADDITIONAL READING

Perhaps the best place to begin further reading is with Lenin's major writings. All of these are readily available in inexpensive paperback editions, all of them are vital parts of the scripture of the world communist movement, and all of them are indispensable guideposts to an understanding of Lenin's thought and politics.

What Is To Be Done? (1902) and *One Step Forward, Two Steps Back* (1904) both called for the highly disciplined Russian Marxist party envisaged by Lenin as necessary to lead the revolution to victory. *Two Tactics of Social Democracy in the Democratic Revolution* (1905) demanded that the revolution against tsarism be carried beyond the attainment of political liberties sought after by the bourgeoisie to a much more egalitarian kind of democracy that could be guaranteed only by a "revolutionary-democratic dictatorship of the proletariat and the peasantry." *Materialism and Empiriocriticism* (1908) was Lenin's doctrinaire and philosophically naive defense of Marxist materialism.

Imperialism: The Highest Stage of Capitalism (1916) looked for an imminent European proletarian revolution, bound to rise out of the horrors of World War I, which Lenin termed the "imperialist war." That war, Lenin indicated, was simply the final one of a whole series of conflicts which the monopoly stage of capitalism's development had made inevitable. According to Lenin, peace could come only with the workers' revolution, with their joining fraternal hands across national boundaries. This view, he believed, the workers of Europe had come to accept after much suffering.

In *State and Revolution: Marxist Teaching about the Theory of the State and the Tasks of the Proletariat in the Revolution* (1917). Lenin explained the need for a dictatorship that was to be established by the workers' revolution. (Marx had used the phrase "dictatorship of the proletariat" but had never made clear what his words meant.) Through the instrument of revolutionary state power, Lenin declared, true democracy would be achieved in stages, the final stage, communism, emerging at the same time as the dissolution of "withering away" of the revolutionary state, a form of power that would no longer be required.

The Proletarian Revolution and the Renegade Kautsky (1918) was Lenin's furious defense of his dictatorship, now in operation, against charges by Kautsky that it violated the democratic precepts of Marxism. Lenin here insisted that a really democratic society could only be attained through a dictatorship that rejected any compromise with bourgeois governmental forms.

Left Wing Communism: An Infantile Disease (1920) was written at a time when Lenin was trying to maintain his equilibrium in Russia and was anxious not to arouse a "re-stabilized" capitalism to attack the Soviet state. It was his response to the communist leaders of Western Europe who wanted momentarily (and in Lenin's opinion prematurely) to stage revolutionary uprisings of the kind he had led in Russia. The phrase "left wing communism" in time came to mean any kind of reckless action by communists that, for the sake of some idealistic principle, would endanger the long run goals of the party of a given country or of the international movement as a whole.

In addition to these major writings, other portions of Lenin's *Collected Works* are well worth consulting. Of the five editions printed to date, the second and third (30 volumes) and the fourth (45 volumes) are available in English.

As suggested in the introduction, Lenin is too large a subject to be treated successfully short of a many-volume biography. Lenin has been treated best by authors who have focused their attention upon limited portions of his life and his wide-ranging activities and have examined these portions within a broad historical framework. Pioneering work on the emergence of Lenin as a Russian Marxist leader has been done by Leopold Haimson, *The Russian Marxists and the Origins of Bolshevism* (Cambridge, Mass., 1955); by Donald Treadgold, *Lenin and His Rivals* (New York, 1955); by Bertram Wolfe, *Three Who Made a Revolution* (New York, 1948); and by Richard Pipes, *Social Demo-*

cracy and the St. Petersburg Labor Movement, 1885 – 1897 Cambridge, Mass., 1963), the "The Origins of Bolshevism: The Intellectual Evolution of Young Lenin," in Richard Pipes, ed., *Revolutionary Russia* (Cambridge, Mass., 1968).

Haimson places Lenin within the developing revolutionary and Marxist movement of the turn of the century and his book is a full-bodied account of both Lenin and the leading Marxists with whom he debated while his ideas were being formed. Treadgold continues and expands the discussion by studying Lenin's program in conjunction with those of competing socialists and liberals through the revolution of 1905 and its aftermath. Wolfe's colorfully written book focuses on the early career of Lenin in his struggle against Menshevism up to 1914. Pipes presents an interesting thesis, suggesting that Lenin arrived at Jacobin political formulations as a result of his awareness that democratic Marxism was not winning the trade-union workers away from their normally moderate and non-revolutionary economic goals. Pipes' thesis has been challenged by Alan K. Wildman in *The Making of a Workers' Revolution: Russian Social Democracy, 1891–1903* (Chicago, 1967).

The mystery that surrounds Lenin's acceptance of German gold during World War I and the famous "sealed train" journey back from exile to Russia are examined in Z.A.B. Zeman, *Germany and the Revolution in Russia, 1915–1918* (London, 1958), in George Katkov, *Russia, 1917* (London, 1967), and in Michael Futrell, *Northern Underground* (London, 1963).

In general, the best material on the final decade of Lenin's life—including World War I, the revolution of 1917, and the grounding of the Soviet state, may be found in the standard works on these periods, among them Olga Gankin and Harold Fisher, *The Bolsheviks in the World War* (Stanford, 1940); Leon Trotsky, *History of the Russian Revolution*, 3 vols. (London, 1932-33); William H. Chamberlin, *The Russian Revolution, 1917–1921*, 2 vols. (New York, 1935), volume 1 of which leans heavily on Trotsky's interpretation of Lenin; John Reed, *Ten Days That Shook the World* (New York, 1934), the "conscientious" but admittedly biased account by an American journalist now buried in the Kremlin cemetery; N. N. Sukhanov, *The Russian Revolution, 1917*, 2 vols. (New York, 1955), an abridgment of the original Russian seven volumes written by a shrewd observer and a prodigious notetaker; Edward Hallet Carr, *The Bolshevik Revolution, 1917–1923*, 3 vols. (New York, 1950-53); Franz Borkenau, *The Communist International* (London, 1938); Louis Fischer, *The Soviets in World Affairs* (London, 1930); and Leonard B. Schapiro, *The Origin of the Communist Autocracy, Political Opposition in the Soviet State, First Phase, 1917–1922* (Cambridge, Mass., 1955). Lenin as an individual is but a shadow in Schapiro's book, but his ominous presence as the ruthless shaper of a government, determined to crush all dissident factions, emerges powerfully from this presentation.

Special insights into Lenin's personality and character may be gained from reading Stanley W. Page, *Lenin and World Revolution* (New York, 1959; Gloucester, 1968); Bertram Wolfe, *The Bridge and the Abyss: The Troubled Friendship of Maxim Gorky and V. I. Lenin* (New York, 1967); Nadezhda Krupskaya, *Memories of Lenin* (London, 1942); Angelica Balabanoff, *Impressions of Lenin* (University of Michigan, 1964); E. Victor Wolfenstein, *The Revolutionary Personality: Lenin, Trotsky, Gandhi* (Princeton, 1967); Nikolai Valentinov, *The Early Years of Lenin* (Ann Arbor, 1969); Stanley W. Page, "Lenin, Turgenev and the Russian Landed Gentry," *Canadian Slavonic Papers*, XVIII, No. 4, December, 1976; Klara Zetkin, *Reminiscences of Lenin* (New York, 1934); Albert Rhys Williams, *Lenin: The Man and His Work* (New York, 1919); and Leonard Schapiro and Peter Reddaway, eds., *Lenin, the Man, the Theorist, the Leader* (New York, 1967).

My own book argues that much of what is known as Leninism grew directly out of Lenin's drive for personal power, particularly his desire to be remembered as the leader of the world revolution. Wolfe's book on Lenin and Gorky is one of the most perceptive treatments of Lenin to date, quite objective, and one of the more dramatic chronicles of the revolution. Krupskaya, Lenin's wife, found no faults in her husband, whether as a person or as a political leader. Still, her completely unadorned, workaday chronicle about her husband as he engaged in routine revolutionary activity is a basic source in any attempt to understand Lenin. Mme. Balabanoff's brief sketch is a personal reaction by a former close associate who broke with Lenin in the early 1920s. Writing in her eightieth year, she had come to regard Lenin as a ruthless and brutal man. Wolfenstein's book contains the first psychobiography of the young Lenin but is much too Freudian. Valentinov's biased memoirs are also designed to cast fresh light on young Lenin's emotions. My article suggests that Lenin's revolutionary fanaticism grew in part out of his ejection from the world of Turgenev's nobles, following upon his brother's execution. Zetkin and Williams each have written a hymn to a living saint. The Schapiro and Reddaway compilation of articles renders Lenin more intelligible than most other books on the subject by analyzing as separate topics many of the segments of his thought and politics. Of particular merit in this collection are the essays by Bohdan R. Bociurkiw, "Lenin and Religion"; John Erickson, "Lenin as Civil War Leader"; Ivo Lapenna, "Lenin, Law and Legality"; and Victor S. Frank, "Lenin and the Russian Intelligentsia."

Among the biographies in English not drawn upon in this book the best is David Shub, *Lenin* (New York, 1948). Shub combines firsthand experiences, as a member of the Russian Social Democratic Party in its formative years, with fairly careful research. The book's objectivity is relatively unmarred by the ideological polarizations of the cold war. Nina Gourfinkle, *Lenin* (New York, 1961) is a brief but well composed and effectively illustrated paperback. George Vernadsky, *Lenin, Red Dictator* (New Haven, 1931) perceives Lenin as one of history's greatest tyrants. René Fülöp-Miller, *Lenin and Gandhi* (New York, 1927) admires Lenin but regrets his use of force. Stephan Possony, *Lenin, the Compulsive Revolutionary* (Chicago, 1964) works hard at sifting underground and police file evidence about Lenin's activities prior to 1914. The second half of the book is less worthwhile because it is taken up with the fruitless task of proving Lenin a German agent. Harold Shukman, *Lenin and the Russian Revolution* (New York, 1967) reviews Lenin's life largely in terms of his efforts to assert his own power over the Bolshevik

party. Shukman describes how the party was molded by Lenin into a perfect instrument of political warfare through the commitment of its members not so much to a set of ideas as to the concept of a Lenin-directed organization as an end in itself.

Among the more useful scholarly articles on Lenin are Stanley W. Page, "Lenin and Self-Determination," *The Slavonic and East European Review*, April, 1950; Robert V. Daniels, "Lenin and the Russian Revolutionary Tradition," *Harvard Slavic Studies*, IV (The Hague, 1957); Alan K. Wildman, "Lenin's Battle with *Kustarnichestvo*; The Iskra Organization in Russia," *Slavic Review*, XXIII, No. 3, Sept., 1964; and Frederick Lilge, "Lenin and the Politics of Education," *Slavic Review*, XVII, No. 2, June, 1968.

Bibliographical surveys on works about Lenin may be found in Walter Laqueur, *The Fate of the Revolution* (London, 1967); Robert D. Warth, "Lenin: The Western Image Forty Years After," *Antioch Review*, XXIV, No. 4, 1964-65, and the same author's "On the Historiography of the Russian Revolution," *Slavic Review*, XXVI, No. 2, June, 1967; and Arthur E. Adams, "New Books on the Revolution—Old Wine in New Bottles," *The Russian Review*, Oct., 1967.

Additional useful information may be found in Alexander Rabinowitch, *Prelude to Revolution: The Petrograd Bolsheviks and the July 1917 Uprising* (Bloomington, 1968); Robert V. Daniels, *Red October; The Bolshevik Revolution of 1917* (New York, 1967); Thomas T. Hammond, *Lenin on Trade Unions and Revolution, 1893—1917* (New York, 1957); Louise Bryant, *Mirrors of Moscow* (New York, 1923); A.F. Ilyin-Genevsky, *From the February to the October Revolution, 1917* (New York, 1931); Robert V. Daniels, *The Conscience of the Revolution* (Cambridge, Mass., 1955); Albert Rhys Williams, *Journey Into Revolution, Petrograd, 1917—1918* (Chicago, 1969); Isaac Deutscher, *Lenin's Childhood*, (London, 1970); Alfred Erich Senn, *The Russian Revolution in Switzerland, 1914—1917* (Madison, Wisc., 1971); Robert H. MacNeal, *Bride of the Revolution, Krupskaya and Lenin* (Ann Arbor, 1972); Saul N. Silverman, *Lenin*, (Englewood Cliffs, N.J., 1972); Stanley W. Page, "Lenin and 'Peasant' Bolshevism," *Journal of Baltic Studies*, III/2, 1972; Rolf

H. Theen, *Lenin, Genesis and Development of a Revolutionary* (Philadelphia, 1973); Leon Trotsky, *Lenin, Notes for a Biographer* (New York, 1973); Robert D. Warth, *Lenin* (New York, 1973); Andrew Ezergailis, *The 1917 Revolution in Latvia* (New York, 1974); Benjamin M. Weissman, *Herbert Hoover and Famine Relief to Soviet Russia, 1921–1923* (Stanford, 1974); Alexander Rabinowitch, *The Bolsheviks Come To Power, the Revolution of 1917 in Petrograd* (New York, 1976); Aleksandr Solzhenitsyn, *Lenin in Zurich* (New York, 1976); Stanley W. Page and Andrew Ezergailis, "The Lenin-Latvian Axis in the Seizure of Power," *Canadian Slavonic Papers,* XIX, No. 1, 1977.

I am happy to mention here a book which appeared just before presstime, which contains numerous articles with fresh interpretations of Lenin by the following authors; Barbara E. Clements, Charles Duval, Herbert Ellison, Andrew Ezergailis, Marc Ferro, Myron W. Hedlin, George D. Jackson, Stanley W. Page, Roger Pethybridge, Michal Reiman, Rex A. Wade and Allan K. Wildman. The book is *Reconsiderations On The Russian Revolution,* edited by Ralph Carter Elwood whose introductory comment is itself extremely valuable. (Cambridge, Mass., 1976.)